Mary's Healthy Vegan Kitchen:

Where healthy eating begins

Cooking Vegan, New Southern style cuisine from scratch on a budget.

Mary's Healthy Vegan Kitchen:

Where healthy eating begins

Cooking Vegan, New Southern style cuisine from scratch on a budget.

Mary Muhammad

In the name of Allah (God) Most gracious, Most merciful

<u>Dedication</u>

I give a heartfelt gratitude to my grandmother and mother who was my first teachers in the kitchen.

Mary's vegan recipes are dedicated to my husband, my children, grandchildren, great grandchildren and all of the people who want better health and to have an alternated lifestyle through the diet.

Eat healthy and enjoy life!

Acknowledgments

With the name of Allah (God), most gracious, most merciful

First, I give thanks to our Creator, who gave me the inspiration and insight to create the recipes for this cookbook.

I want to offer a special thanks to my mother, Mrs. Alice Lounday - Matthews and my grandmother, Mrs. Neater "Feet" Matthews, who introduced me to cooking at an early age in the "Ridge," Patterson, Georgia.

I wish to thank my daughter, Emma who was my critic, taster and shared some of her recipes with me to convert to vegan recipes.

I wish to thank my son Clarence and his friends and my friends who were brave enough to test my recipes.

Many thanks to my friend, Zarinah M. El-Amin who trusted me with some of her recipes to be converted to vegan recipes.

A special thanks to my husband, Muslim "Shabazz" Muhammad who enjoys my cooking and also gave me encouragement to write this cookbook.

List of contents

Guide to food index

Breakfast entrees

Sandwiches & burgers

Smoothies & appetizers

Awesome avocado and fruit smoothie	16
Energizing green smoothie	24
Exotic fruit smoothie	25
Mixed fruit smoothie	37
Avocado dip	71
Baked spicy and cheesy potatoes	81
Chick less flavored tofu strips	100
Power pack green smoothie	286

Main dishes

Savory Garbanzo beans	49
Savory lentil beans and mushroom	51
Delicious spicy mushroom meat loaf	53
Delightful dirty couscous	61
Garbanzo beans Meat less chili	65
Grilled barbeque tofu steak	68
Baked almond tofu steaks	79
Spicy baked barbeque tofu steaks	83

Lovely breads, pie crusts and muffins

Soups, broth & salads

Flavorful carrots & tomato noodle soup	20
Raw is better kale salad	42
Raw supreme carrot "mock tuna" salad	46
Hearty angel hair nests vegetable soup	70
Awesome carrot "tuna" salad & pasta	123
Egg-less picnic potato salad	125
Gourmet vegan salad	136
Green energy salad	145
Hearty and bold old fashion vegetarian soup	153
Hearty vegetables, tofu and red potato soup	156
Fantastic navy bean soup	185
Raw supreme carrot "mock tuna" salad	190
Spicy vegan black bean soup	218
Gluten free tofu pumpkin seed salad	245
Vegetable broth	259
Canadian speckle beans dump soup	282

Pasta dishes

Vegan macaroni and cheese	35
Awesome carrot "tuna" salad & pasta	77
Broccoli and pasta with gold sauce	96
Creamy southern flair macaroni and cheese	107

Rice & grains

Gold rice	29
Delightful dirty couscous	61
Cooked long grain basmati brown rice	104
Healthy whole grain millet	150
Nutty flavored quinoa	270
Red beans and rice	280

Salad dressings, sauces & gravies

Gold Sauce	31
Homemade orange BBQ sauce	33
Creamy carrot supreme salad dressing	39
Raw garlic and tomato salad dressing	41

Frostings & Baked deserts

Miscellaneous

"And seek help through patience and prayer." (Quran 2:45)

Introduction

I have always been more interested in eating vegetables, bread and sweets rather than eating meat, even when I was growing up in the rural South (Georgia). Growing up in the "Ridge," on my uncle's farm was fun and work. We had lots of pecan trees, watermelons and all the food we wanted to eat. I didn't grow up thinking that we were poor, even though I lived with my grandmother in a little house sitting back in the woods. All the neighbors lived the same way and they all helped each other. My grandmother was always making good smells come from her kitchen.

I would watch my grandmother and my mother cook different kinds of food and sometimes they would let me help cook. They would cook collards, mustards and other vegetables. But I really liked cooking deserts and became really good with making cakes. In 1951 my mother moved to Florida to live. About 5 years later, my grandmother became ill and had to go up north to live with her daughter. Consequently, I moved to Florida to live with my mother. I missed the county but I made friends. After school, I continued to make desert by making coconut candy for me and my friend and because we had a coconut tree in the yard.

My interest in cooking continued all though my high school days. I would bake a cake for my nephew's birthday and anyone else who asked. But I still loved cooking mainly vegetables like collards, mustards, turnips, corn and cabbage, as well as some meats. I didn't know about broccoli, kale and the many other kinds of healthy vegetables at that time.

Later in my life, after a divorce, my children and I moved to Decatur, Georgia. I met my present husband in 1978 and I became a Muslim in 1979 and my husband and I married that same year. Then one day my husband and I went to hear Dr. Paul Goss's lecture that was held at Sister Clara Muhammad School in Atlanta, Georgia. This was the eye opener that I needed because I had to find a new way to prepare our meals. I started to do some research after my husband had a reflux attack that landed in him the hospital. In addition, I was overweight. I weighed about 200 pounds. I started to look at a new way of changing the way I cooked our meals and what we ate.

However, we were still eating meat at that time, but no pork. I learned about broccoli and many other kinds of healthy vegetables and began to cook them. I started to experiment so much in the kitchen with different vegetables dishes and whole grains that my husband would request by jokingly asking: "What's cooking in Mary's kitchen?" I tried different bean dishes and one of my friends told me about using cream of wheat to make bread because it is easier to digest than cornmeal. So consequently, I started using cream of wheat. I would ask questions to Vegetarians, especially those in health food stores. At the farmers market I learned about the different spices and herbs from different countries and found so many vegetarian items that was available. I stopped buying items that had hydrogenated oils in them. I started to make my own salad dressings and cooking from scratch in a new southern way, so I could control the ingredients. I started to buy organic and natural foods because these farmers work in harmony to maintain healthy fertile soil without chemicals and additives. I began to read the labels before I bought an item. We began to eat lots of fruits, vegetables and whole grains such as quinoa, couscous, millet, black rice and a variety of seed such as sunflower seeds, pumpkin seeds, celery seeds and flaxseeds. I lost weight and my husband's reflux improved as we began to eat healthy.

In 1992 my husband and I decided to officially become Vegetarians and my recipes were converted to vegetarian-style recipes. I began to experiment with tofu and later on I tried (top) textured vegetable protein. We had been vegetarians for 6 years before we became Vegans in 1998. At that time I was inspired to write this cookbook because of my husband experiences with reflux and myself being overweight. This has been over 12 years ago and my husband does not have the reflux anymore and we both have lost weight eating a vegan diet.

Today, I don't overcook my vegetables and I use spices that are healthy and good for the whole body in my recipes such as fennel, turmeric, ginger and cayenne pepper, to name a few. I use extra virgin olive or grape seed oils in my cooking and lots of my recipes are gluten free.

I hope you will enjoy these vegan recipes that I have lovingly prepared, to help improve our health, mind, body and spirit. I have used natural and organic products in my recipes along with spring water. No preservatives, dairy, eggs, animal ingredients, commercial white sugar or enriched white flour are found in my recipes. So explore and experiment with me because fresh vegetables and fruits are very easy to find today; there are numerous health food stores, farmers markets and grocery stores that carry healthy items. Most importantly, read labels before buying your food AND IF YOU DON'T KNOW WHAT THE WORDS, MEAN DON'T BUY!!
Because to be healthy is to be wealthy!

"Our food should be our medicine. Our medicine should be our food." Hippocrates

Cooking tips that I have learned from my years of cooking

1. To slice bell peppers easily, turn bell pepper so the inside is facing you and slice.
2. Ground fresh, whole flaxseed in high-speed blender and store in refrigerator.
3. Flaxseeds are very healthy with omega 3. They can be sprinkled on cereals, yogurt, smoothies and cooked in baked goods.
4 Kelp is a healthy variety of seaweed and can be used to give a fish taste to different dishes.
5. Organic turmeric is used to add a natural color to foods and have many health benefits.
6. To replace an egg, use 1 tablespoon of flaxseeds plus 3 tablespoons spring water for each egg. 1/3 cup of unsweetened apple sauce can also be used to replace one egg.
7. 1-1/2 teaspoon egg replacer and 2 tablespoons of spring water replaces one egg.
8. For milder chili omit cayenne pepper and season individual bowls with a sprinkle of cayenne pepper.
9. To peel tomatoes, cover them with boiling hot water for 5 minutes then poke with the knife and peel.
10. To make almond milk, put 1-cup sliced almonds and 1-cup spring water in heavy-duty blender and ground on high speed for 2-minutes then strain with a piece of cheese cloth to get out the almond residue, leaving the milk.
11. For quicker cooking Basmati rice, soak rice in spring water for 10 minutes at room temperature then rinse before cooking.
12. Do not add water to anything that has scorched or burned. Just take out the part that is not burned and put in a clean pot, add a little water to the clean pot and continue cooking.
13. To peel mushrooms, start at the top and peel downward.

14. To separate garlic cloves, sit the garlic on its flat bottom and give a tap on the top of the head with the palm of the hand or a flat heavy object.

15. Never put cold water in a hot glass. Baking dishes always require hot water.

16. Let bake goods cool completely before frosting.

17. Spray scooper with non-stick organic olive oil spray to easily transfer burger to fry pan or cookie mixture to cookie sheet.

18. Invest in good quality stainless steel pots and pans and non-stick pans

19. Always have all ingredients/utensils and cooking pans, pots laid out and prepared before starting

20. Prepare cake pans before making a recipe

21. Grease well and/or line cake pans, cookie sheets with parchment paper and spray lightly with non-stick spray. This makes the removal and cleaning easier.

22. Soak beans in 2 qt of water and 1 teaspoon aluminum free baking soda for cleaner alkaline water to soak beans and to get rid of gas from beans.

23. Always use extra virgin cold-pressed olive oil in recipes; it can be used in baking as well.

24. Wash dishes at intervals to keep cooking area clean

25. Never cook food in aluminum foil pans and when covering items with aluminum foil, always use parchment paper next to food.

26. Soak non-organic vegetables in white vinegar and water for 10 minutes to rid vegetables of pesticides

Measurements

1 Tbsp = 3 tsp

2 Tbsp= 6 tsp

1/4 c=4 tbsp

1/3c=5 tbsp

1/2c =8 tbs

1 pound=16oz

1oz=2 tbsp (dry)

1 liter=4c plus 3 1/2tbsp

1 quart=4 c

1 pint=2 c

1c= 8 oz

1/2c= 4 oz

½ gallon= 9-1/2 cups

1 gallon= 16 cups

2/3c =5oz

3/4c =6oz

Essentials for good health

1. Pray daily
2. Drink an 16oz glass of water (spring water if available) upon rising in the morning
3. Buy fresh flaxseeds at the market and ground a portion in a high speed blender and put in covered jar and store both flaxseeds in refrigerator
4. Soak fruits/ vegetables in1/2 gallon water and 1 tbsp aluminum free baking soda to alkaline the water and get items clean
5. Soak dried beans in enough water to cover them and 1 tsp aluminum free baking soda overnight, rinse thoroughly store in refrigerator in portion containers
6. After soaking beans use amount the recipe calls for and freeze the rest.
7. Never leave cooked food sitting on the counter for long periods of time
8. Eat a colorful salad daily
9. Never over cook vegetables
10. Use organic sprouted tofu for better health
11. Wash hands before cooking or eating

Almond coated navy bean burger

Makes about 12 medium burgers. Preparation Time: 30 minutes.

Cooking Time: 40 minutes. Total time: 1hour + 10 minutes

Description: Baked, savory and with a crunchy top. I always cook up lots of beans and freeze them so I will always have them on hand. I bake these burgers when I am in a hurry and they are awesome.

INGREDIENTS:

3cups cooked drained navy beans

2 tablespoons grounded flax seeds

5 tablespoons bean liquid

1/2 purple onion

3 fresh garlic cloves

1 carrot

1/2 red bell pepper

3 tablespoons liquid amino

1/4 teaspoon cayenne pepper

1/2 teaspoon grounded paprika

1/2cup grounded gluten free oats

1 cup cooked quinoa, see pg. 270

1-1/2 cups grounded raw almonds

1/2 cup cold pressed olive oil

Non-stick organic olive oil spray

1 gallon spring water

1 teaspoon aluminum free baking soda for soaking beans

Small piece of rinsed ginger

DIRECTIONS:

Cooking the beans:

First, pick out any small rocks or debris then soak in spring water and 1 teaspoon aluminum -free baking soda overnight then drain and rinse well. (Quick soak follow directions on bag). Cook the navy beans uncovered in 1 cup water on high heat to boil then turn heat to medium/low add 5 cups of water, ginger. Cover pot and cook for 1-1/2 hours until tender then drain off the liquid and save and measure out 3 cups. Proceed to make burgers.

Grind the almonds in the food processor very fine and set aside.

Grind the oats in the food processor very fine and set aside.

Peel and wash the vegetables and cut them in small piece and set aside

Mix 5 tablespoons of bean liquid and flaxseed together to gel.

Mash 3 cups of navy beans and flaxseed mixture in the food processor and put in a medium bowl. It is okay to leave a few beans half mashed.

Chop the onion and bell pepper fine with a knife and put in the bowl.

Chop the garlic and carrot in food processor and add to the bowl, add liquid amino, cayenne pepper and quinoa. Stir well.

Gently toss the grounded almond and oats lightly into the burger mixture.

Put 4 tablespoons oil in large heavy duty non-stick skillet on top of the stove and turn the heat to medium. Use a large ice cream scooper sprayed with non-stick olive oil spray to scoop the burger mix and place into the pan. Only place 4 burgers in the pan at a time and cook 4 minutes. Then turn the burger over and press lightly with the back of the solid pancake turner sprayed with non-stick spray and cook for 4 minutes on each side or until both sides are brown. Continue cooking until all burgers are cooked. Add small amount of oil and spray pancake turner as needed. Serve on a bun with your favorite toppings.

Preheat oven to 400 degrees.

These burgers can be baked in a large oblong baking pan sprayed with non-stick spray. Stir the 1/4 cup olive oil into the mix and with an ice-cream scooper that has been sprayed with non-stick spray and drop burgers into the pan and press lightly with the back of the flipper and bake 400 degrees for 40 minutes. If tops are not browned, turn oven to broil to brown but watch carefully. Allow to sit for 5 minutes before serving.

Preparation items: large bowl, food processor, measuring cup and spoons, large spoon, knife and cutting board, non-stick skillet and oblong baking pan, ice-cream scooper, solid pancake flipper and parchment paper.

Apple ginger cake squares

Serves: 15.   Preparation Time: 15 minutes

Cooking time: 35 minutes. Total Time: 50 minutes

Description: These squares can be served with soy whipped cream on top or frost with creamy applesauce drizzle. These squares are moist and not too sweet.

INGREDIENTS:

3cups spelt flour

2teaspoons aluminum free baking powder

1/4teaspoon sea salt

1/2 teaspoon aluminum -free baking soda

1 tablespoon ground ginger

1- 3/4 cups turbinino cane sugar in the raw

1cup Easy homemade applesauce page 7

1 tablespoon blond grounded flaxseeds

3 tablespoons spring water

1 cup almond milk

1 tablespoon fresh lemon juice

1 cup walnut pieces

1 cup earth balance margarine

1 can organic non-stick olive oil spray

DIRECTIONS:

Preheat oven 350 degree

Line the baking pan with parchment paper and spray lightly.

Crush the walnuts in food processor and save 1/3 cup for frosting.

Mix the milk and lemon juice and set aside.

Mix flaxseeds and water together and set aside.

Mix well the flour, baking powder, salt, baking soda and ginger and set aside in a large bowl.

In a blender, blend the sugar, applesauce and margarine, the flaxseed mixture, lemon and milk mixture and mix lightly until creamy.

Add the wet mixture gradually to the dry ingredients. Mix with large mixing spoon.

Continue mixing until the wet and dry ingredients are mixed in.

Fold in the nuts.

Pour into prepared pan and shake the pan to even out the batter.

Bake for 35 minutes or until tooth pick inserted comes out clean. If wet comes out on toothpick, bake cake for 3-5 minutes more and re-test.

Let cake rest in pan for 10 minutes. The move to a plate and remove the parchment paper. Cool completely before frosting with applesauce drizzle or cutting into squares. Sprinkle crushed walnuts on top of frosting.

Optional: Applesauce drizzle frosting

Variety: 1 cup agave nectar can be used but reduce the milk by 4 tablespoons.

Preparation items: oblong non-stick baking pan, measuring cup and spoons, mixing spoon, 2 large bowl, 2 cups, high speed blender, paring knife.

Crushed apple cream frosting

Frost one cake. Preparation Time: 10 minutes. Mixing Time: 5 minutes. Total Time: 15 minutes

Description: Very nice buttery apple taste

INGREDIENTS:

5 cups organic confections sugar; add more if needed.

1/2tablespoon soft earth balance spread

2 teaspoons alcohol -free vanilla flavor

1/2 cup well-drained easy unsweetened homemade applesauce

Chop the pecans in the food processor and set aside.

In a large bowl, mix the confections sugar, earth balance spread, vanilla Flavor and stir.

Add the drained applesauce and beat with electric mixer until creamy. If the frosting is too thick, add a drop of almond milk until desired consistency.

Sprinkle the chopped pecans on top of frosted item if desired.

Easy unsweetened homemade applesauce

Preparation items: large bowl, stirring spoon, measuring cups and spoons, food processor.

Easy homemade unsweetened applesauce

Yield: 1 cup. Preparation time: 5 minutes. Cooking time: 25 minutes
Total time: 30 minutes.

Description: Delicious and easy to digest and can be used in any recipe
calling for unsweetened applesauce.

INGREDIENTS:

2 gala apples, peeled and cored

2 cups spring water

2 thin slices of organic lemons

DIRECTIONS:

Cut apples in small pieces and put in sauce pan with the water on top of
the stove and cook on medium heat until apples are very soft. Take out
lemons and drain liquid and mash apples with a potato masher or food
processor. Now you have applesauce!

Variety: 1/2 teaspoon of cinnamon can be added to the apple sauce.

Preparation items: small pot, spoon, potato masher, knife, food
processor and cutting board.

Awesome avocado and fruit smoothie

Yield: 6 cups. Preparation time: 5 minutes. Blending time: 3 minutes. Total time: 8 minutes

Description: Awesome fruit and avocado smoothie that is smooth and refreshing.

INGREDIENTS:

1/2 peeled ripe deseeded avocado

1 ripe banana

2 cups frozen strawberries

2 tablespoons grounded flax seeds

1 cup frozen papaya

4 tablespoons pure maple syrup

2 tablespoons grounded sunflower seeds

2-1/2 cups spring water

DIRECTIONS:

Put the avocado, banana, 1/2 of the frozen strawberries, one cup of water and flaxseeds in heavy duty blender.

Grind on high speed until smooth and creamy. Add the rest of strawberries, 1 cup of water and continue to grind until smooth. Add the frozen papaya, 1/2 cup water and grind until smooth and creamy.

Add sweetener, sunflower seeds and grind until creamy. Taste and add more sweetener and water if needed.

Preparation items: heavy duty blender, measuring cups and spoons, knife and cutting board.

Black Bean Burger

Yield: 12 burgers. Preparation Time: 25minutes. Cooking time: 40 minutes. Total time: 1hour + 5 minutes

Description: Healthy baked alternate burger with lots of fiber and delicious. I always cook up lots of beans and freeze them so I will always have them on hand.

INGREDIENTS:

3 cups cooked drained black beans

Save the bean liquid for later

1-1/2cups raw sunflower seeds

1stalks celery

1/2 onion

4 garlic cloves

1/2 red bell pepper

2tablespoons flaxseeds

5 tablespoons bean liquid

1-1/2 cups cooked millet

4 tablespoons olive oil

1/4 teaspoon cayenne pepper

1 teaspoon turmeric

1 teaspoon grounded fennel

1 teaspoon chili powder

2 tablespoons Bragg's liquid amino

2 tablespoon Follow your heart original vegenaise sandwich spread

1 can of organic non-stick spray

1 teaspoon aluminum- free baking powder for soaking beans

Small piece fresh ginger

1 gallon spring water

DIRECTIONS:

Cooking the beans:

First, pick out any small rocks or debris in the beans. Then soak in spring water with 1 teaspoon of aluminum - free baking soda overnight. Then drain and rinse well. (For Quick soak, follow directions on bag) Sauté the black beans in 1 cup of water and a small piece of ginger on high heat to boil, turn heat to medium/low and add 5 cups water and cook for 2 hours until tender. Then drain the liquid and save. Measure out 3 cups and proceed to make burgers.

Preheat oven to 400 degrees and spray baking pan with organic non-stick spray. Grind sunflower seeds to a course meal and set aside.

Clean the vegetables and chop them in food processor.

Soak flaxseeds in bean liquid for 5 minutes.

Mash beans and soaked flaxseeds well in the food processor and put in a large bowl.

Sauté the vegetables in 2 tablespoons oil for 1 minute then add to the bean mix. Mix in millet, flour, oil, seasonings, sandwich spread and mix well.

Fold in the grounded sunflower seed and mix lightly. Use a large ice-cream scooper sprayed with non-stick olive oil spray to scoop the burger mix and place burgers into the prepared pan and flatten lightly with the back of the flipper sprayed with non-stick olive oil spray.

These big Burgers can be baked in the oven at 400 degrees for 40 minutes. Flatten lightly before baking. Bake until burgers are light brown. Let burgers sit for 5 minutes then serve on a bun with sandwich spread, vegan cheese, lettuce, tomato slice, onion and pickle.

Preparation items: large plate, oblong large stainless steel pan, measuring spoons and cups, large bowl, food processor and ice cream scooper, tablespoon solid pancake flipper and cutting board.

Flavorful carrots & tomato noodle soup

Serves: 8. Preparation Time: 14 minutes. Cooking Time: 40 minutes
Total Time: 54 minutes

Description: This soup is light and flavorful and really is prefect for a
light lunch-time meal.

INGREDIENTS:

2-large tomatoes

1/2 onions

3 fresh cloves garlic

2 carrots

1/2 of fresh red bell pepper

5 fresh string beans

2 tablespoons vegan margarine

1 teaspoon powdered paprika

1 teaspoon basil

1/4 teaspoon thyme

1/8 Tsp cayenne pepper powder

3 squirts fructose and gluten free ketchup

1 tablespoon powdered vegetable broth mix and 4 tablespoons spring water mixed well

9cups spring water

1 teaspoon maple syrup

3 Bay leaves

5 sticks of gluten free spaghetti broken into small section

1/4 teaspoon sea salt add last and to taste

DIRECTIONS:

Peel the garlic and wash and rinse all vegetables and set aside.

Put the tomatoes in the food processor along with the garlic, onions and ground well.

Slice the carrots.

Cube the bell pepper and cut ends off string beans and cut in small pieces.

Add all prepared vegetables, oil and all of the dry seasonings to the pot.

Turn the heat to medium and sauté for 5 minutes.

Stir in the vegetable broth mixture, 8 cups of water to the pot.

Turn on the heat to high and let soup come to a quick boil on top of the stove.

Then turn the heat to medium and add the ketchup, bay leaves and cook for 35 minutes

Add the small broken spaghetti; add a portion at a time and stir. When all of the spaghetti is added, add last cup of water.

Stir often to keep the spaghetti from sticking together.

Add the maple syrup and continue cooking for 5 minutes or more if needed for spaghetti to get soft. Take out the bay leaves, stir and taste. You may add salt if needed.

Turn off heat and serve hot.

*Preparation items: large heavy stainless steel pot with lid, stirring spoon, cutting board, measuring cups and spoons, medium bowl and food processor.

Down home candied sweet potatoes

Serves: 6. Preparation Time: 15 minutes. Cooking Time: 40 minutes. Total Time: 55 minutes

Description: Sweet potatoes come in different colored skins and they are packed with healthy nutrients. These candied potatoes are orange in color, sweet, flavorful and all natural and taste good.

INGREDIENTS:

4 medium sweet potatoes

1 cup of spring water

1 teaspoon ground cinnamon

1/2 teaspoon ground nutmeg

2 teaspoons vanilla flavor

1/2 cup earth balance spread melted

2 tablespoons fresh lemon juice

1 cup raw maple syrup

Note: 6 packs stevia in the raw and 1/2 cup maple syrup can be used if desired

DIRECTIONS:

Scrub the potatoes clean with a clean cloth and water and scrap off blemishes.

Peel and slice the potatoes in medium round slices.

Rinse well and put the potatoes and water in the pan and cover and let them steam on medium /low heat for 20 minutes.

Put the spices, flavor, melted earth balance, lemon juice and maple syrup in a small bowl and stir well to incorporate. Then pour half of the mixture over the potatoes and turn potatoes over with a plastic pancake turner and pour the other half of spice mixture over it.

Continue to cook uncovered on top of the stove on medium/low heat for 20 minutes or until the potatoes are tender and the juice thickens a little.

Dip some of the juice over the potatoes when serving.

Preparation items: medium pot with lid, measuring cup and spoons, medium plastic turner, small spoon, potato peeler, chopping board and sharp knife.

*For variation: Raisins can be added during the last part of the cooking process if desired.

Energizing green smoothie

Yield: 4 cups. Preparation time: 5 minutes. Mixing Time: 5 minutes. Total time: 10 minutes

Description: creamy and energizing

INGREDIENTS:

5 kale stems, fresh or frozen

6 cubes of frozen papaya

1 ripe banana

Small core of purple cabbage

2 cups spring water

Small handful of raw walnuts

2 teaspoons of raw pumpkin seeds

1 small fresh turmeric peeled

4 pitted medjool dates if sweetener is desired

DIRECTIONS:

Put first 4 items in the blender, add water and blend on high speed until creamy. Add the last 4 items and continue to blend on high speed until creamy. If too thick, add a little water until desired thickness is obtained.

Preparation items: measuring cups and spoons, sharp knife, heavy duty blender.

Exotic fruit smoothie

Serves: 4. Preparation Time: 3 minutes. Mixing time: 3 minutes. Total Time: 6 minutes

Description: creamy and is a great morning breakfast or anytime snack.

INGREDIENTS:

1-1/2 cups fresh papaya

1 fresh and peeled kiwi

1/2 cup watermelon

2 ripe bananas

1/2 cup spring water

2 packs stevia in the raw or 4 medjool pitted dates

2 tablespoons raw pumpkin seed

2 tablespoons grounded flax seeds

5 cubed ice

DIRECTIONS:

Peel and clean the fruit and cut into pieces small enough to fit in blender, add the water, 2 cubes of the ice, flax seeds and pumpkin seeds and blend until fruit is broken down. Then add balance of ice, stevia and blend until creamy and smooth.

Smoothie yield about 4-1/2 cups to enjoy

Preparation items: measuring cups and spoons, sharp knife, heavy duty blender and cutting board.

Splendid flaky Pie crust

Yield 2 small pie crusts or 1 large pie crust.

Preparation Time: 30 minutes mixing Time 5 minutes Total Time: 35 minutes

Description: tender and flaky pie crust

INGREDIENTS:

2cups spelt flour

2tablespoons turbinino cane sugar

1/2 stick (4 oz) of cold vegan margarine

1/4cup earth balance vegan shortening

2tablespoons cold almond milk

3tablespoons cold spring water

1 teaspoon fresh lemon juice

DIRECTIONS:

Whisk the flour and sugar together in a large bowl.

Slice the margarine and shortening before adding to the flour mixture.

Use pastry cutter to incorporate the flour mixture and earth balance pieces together until mixture are course and crumbly.

Mix together the lemon juice, cold water and cold milk then pour a little at a time to the crumbly mixture until the mixture can hold together in a round mound. Add small amount of flour if needed.

Then divide the dough into too portions in separate bowls if making two small pies. Put dough in the refrigerator for 30 minutes. (If making one pie crust 9 inch don't separate)

Take one bowl of dough out of refrigerator and place on cleaned counter top sprinkled with flour. Sprinkle flour on top of dough and with a dough roller and roll lightly into a round circle. Use more flour if needed.

Then place into a pie pan on top of rolled crust and flip onto the pie pan an even out. Shave off excess dough or tuck under.

Use the same steps and roll the other half of dough.

Press the edges of crust all around the pan with a floured fork.

Always prepare pie crust first.

Preparation items needed: pie plates, rolling pin, large rolling sheet or wax paper, measuring cups and spoons, pastry cutter, knife and fork.

Gold rice

Serves: 8. Preparation Time: 6 minutes. Cooking Time: 30 minutes.
Total Time: 36 minutes

Description: I had fun with this rice, learning how to prefect it. This
rice has a nutty taste and the gold color is splendid and it is gluten free

INGREDIENTS:

1 cup organic Long grain Basmati Brown rice

1/2 gallon spring water

1/4teaspoon sea salt

4dried whole bay leaves or fresh

2-1/2teaspoons grounded turmeric

2 tablespoons extra virgin olive oil

Dash of grounded cayenne pepper

DIRECTIONS:

1- Soak the rice in 2 cups of water for 6 minutes. This will make the rice cook quicker.

2- After the soaking period, drain the water and add 2 cups of fresh water along with the turmeric, sea salt, cayenne pepper and olive oil and stir well.

Put the uncovered pot on top of the stove on high heat and bring to a quick boil takes about 4 minutes.

3-Then turn the heat to low and let the rice cook on low heat covered for 30 minutes.

Do not open the pot or stir during this process.

4- When the time is up, check a grain of the rice for the firmness you desire. If needed, add a small amount of water and continue to steam until rice is tender.

5-Turn the heat off and keep pot covered for 5 minutes.

Fluff up the rice and take out the bay leaves.

This dish is good served as a side dish with the basil steamed cabbage page 86

Preparation items: medium heavy stainless steel pot, strainer, measuring cups and spoons and fork.

Gold Sauce

Serves: 6. Preparation Time: 8 minutes. Cooking Time: 10 minutes
Total Time: 18 minutes

Description: Colorful sauce and looks and taste good wherever a sauce
is needed.

INGREDIENTS:

1 cup almond milk

1-1/2 teaspoons turmeric

3 tablespoons liquid amino

1/2 teaspoon garlic powder

1/8 teaspoon cayenne pepper

1/4 teaspoon ground thyme

1/2 teaspoon extra virgin olive oil

2 tablespoons pure maple syrup

1-1/2 tablespoons gluten free potato starch mixed with 1/2 cup almond
milk

DIRECTIONS:

Put all of the above ingredients in a medium pot and with a large wooden spoon stir constantly.

Cook for 10 minutes or until creamy; stir while cooking.

Taste and add more seasoning if desired. Remove from the heat and strain sauce then pour over cooked pasta and broccoli or wherever a sauce is needed

Preparation items: medium stainless steel pot, stirring spoon, small holed mesh strainer, measuring cup and spoons.

Homemade orange BBQ sauce

Yield: about 1 pint. Preparation Time: 10 minutes. Cooking Time: 55 minutes. Total Time: 1 hour +5 minutes

Description: This gluten-free barbeque sauce is spicy and tastes good on meat substitutes.

INGREDIENTS:

3 cups of Rega gluten-free organic tomato puree

3/4cup 100% pure gluten free Canadian maple syrup

3tablespoons pure gluten free organic molasses

3-roma tomatoes rinsed chopped

1 small fresh onion peeled rinsed and chopped fine

4 fresh garlic cloves peeled rinsed and chopped fine

1 small fresh jalapeno pepper (take out most of the seeds for less fire)

1/8 teaspoon grounded hot chipotle pepper

3tablespoons grounded smoked paprika

2tablespoons extra virgin olive oil

1 cup fresh orange juice

1/2cup Bragg's apple cider vinegar

3 tablespoons Bragg's liquid amino

DIRECTIONS:

Put tomatoes, onion, jalapeno pepper and garlic in the food processor and chop very fine.

In a medium pot, add oil, chopped veggies and sauté on medium heat 5 minutes.

While the veggies are simmering, add the dry ingredients and stir well.

Add tomato puree, orange juice, liquid amino, vinegar and molasses and stir well.

Continue to cook covered on medium heat for 20 minutes.

Add the maple syrup and mix well.

Turn heat to low and simmer on low heat for 30 minutes or until sauce is bubbly.

Watch the sauce carefully so it won't burn.

Taste and add more seasoning if needed.

When the sauce is cooled, blend in blender until smooth.

This barbeque sauce can be stored in the refrigerator in a closed jar for 2 weeks.

Preparation items: medium stainless steel pot with lid, large stirring spoon, measuring cups and spoons, sharp knife, cutting board and Heavy duty blender.

Vegan macaroni and cheese

Serves:10. Preparation Time:15 minutes. Cooking Time: 30 minutes
Total Time: 45 minutes

Description: Very cheesy and delicious.

INGREDIENTS:

16 ounce box organic macaroni

1-10 ounce block of vegan daiya cheddar style cheese

1-package vegan daiya mozzarella style cheese shreds

3 slices toasted spelt bread

Pinch of cayenne pepper

1/8 teaspoon sea salt optional

1/4cup earth balance natural buttery spread

1 teaspoon powdered paprika

1/2 teaspoon grounded turmeric

4cups original almond milk

DIRECTIONS:

Preheat oven to 400 degrees

In the food processor, ground the cheese very fine and set aside

Grind the bread in the food processor enough for a cup full and mix the crumbs with half of earth balance spread and set aside

Follow directions on the box but cook for about 8 minutes

Use recipe for the cheese sauce on. While the macaroni is cooking make the sauce. When the cheese sauce start to bubble turn off heat.

Stir and drain macaroni in colander. Put the hot macaroni in large bowl and add the ground cheese to the hot macaroni and stir, then add half of the earth balance spread, cheese sauce and all of the other ingredients to the hot macaroni and mix well.

Taste and add more seasoning if needed. Pour into large deep baking dish. Sprinkle the paprika and mozzarella cheese shreds and buttered bread crumbs over the top of the macaroni. Bake for 30 minutes or until it begins to bubble and then take out of oven to serve hot

Preparation items: 1-large pot, measuring spoons, measuring cup, large deep baking dish, large bowl, knife and food processor.

Mixed fruit smoothie

Serves: 5. Preparation Time: 5 minutes. Blending Time: 5 minutes.
Total Time: 10 minutes.

Description: colorful and refreshing healthy smoothie

INGREDIENTS:

1 cup peeled, fresh pineapple

1 cup fresh frozen cantaloupe and few seeds

2 cups spring water

2 medium pieces fresh coconut

1-1/2 fresh bananas

1 cup fresh strawberries

1/2 cup blueberries fresh, frozen

1 tablespoon grounded flaxseeds

2 packs stevia in the raw or

2 tablespoon pure maple syrup

DIRECTIONS:

Cut tops off strawberries and soak strawberries for 5 minutes in cool water, then rinse.

Peel bananas and wash fresh fruits

Fill the blender with 1/2 of the fruit and add half of the water and blend until the fruit is broken down. Then add the remaining fruit, fresh coconut, stevia, maple syrup and flaxseeds and continue blending the fruit on high speed until creamy. If the smoothie is too thick, add a little water and blend well.

Serve at once or store in refrigerator. Smoothie will last for 2 days in refrigerator

Preparation items: heavy duty blender, measuring spoons and cups, 8-4oz glasses

If the smoothie is too thick, add a little water. Then Enjoy!!

* Use organic fruits if available

Raw creamy carrot supreme salad dressing

Yield:16 oz. Preparation Time: 5 minutes. blending Time: 3 minutes. Total Time: 8 minutes.

Description: I decided to make my own salad dressings and I experimented a lot and came up with my own delicious dressings that are low in sodium and made with raw fresh veggies and are healthy.

INGREDIENTS:

1/2cup Organic cold press olive oil

1/4cup Bragg's apple cider vinegar

1 small garlic clove peeled and rinsed

Small piece purple onion peeled and rinsed

1/2 stalk of fresh celery rinsed and cut in small pieces

1 medium carrot rinsed and cut in very small pieces

1 teaspoon paprika powder

Dash of cayenne pepper

2 tablespoons grounded brown flaxseeds

1 teaspoon poppy seeds

3 tablespoons of agave nectar or sweetener of choice

1 cup spring water

1/4teaspoon real sea salt or to taste

DIRECTIONS:

Ground the flaxseeds in a high speed blender. Take out 2 tablespoons of flaxseeds and put leftover flaxseeds in a jar and store in the refrigerator.

Put all ingredients in a heavy duty blender and blend on high speed for 3minutes.

Add half of the water and blend until creamy.

Take the remaining half of the water and rinse out the blender and pour the dressing into the container.

Shake well and refrigerate.

If dressing is too thick, add a little water until desired thickness and shake.

Maple syrup, raw sugar or any sweetener can be used.

Preparation items: heavy duty blender, measuring spoons and cups, knife, pint size container with lid

Raw garlic and tomato salad dressing

Yield:16 oz. Preparation Time: 5 minutes. Blending Time: 3 minutes. Total Time: 8 minutes.

Description: This is another one of my made from scratch raw salad dressings that is delicious and have healthy nutrients and is quick and easy.

INGREDIENTS

1 large fresh tomato cubed small

1 garlic peeled and rinsed

Small piece of purple onion peeled and rinsed

1/2cup extra virgin olive oil

1/4cup Bragg's apple cider vinegar

1/2 teaspoon paprika

1/2teaspoon whole basil flakes

1/8 teaspoon cayenne pepper

2 tablespoons grounded flax seeds

1 cup cold spring water

2 teaspoons Bragg's liquid amino or 1/4 teaspoon real sea salt

3 +tablespoons light agave nectar or to taste

DIRECTIONS:

Put all ingredients in a heavy-duty blender and half of the water along with all of the above ingredients and blend for 3 minutes on high speed until the mixture is creamy.

Taste and add more seasoning if needed.

Pour the salad dressing into a pint size container.

Take the remaining water and rinse out the blender and pour the liquid into the jar and shake well to mix.

Preparation items: heavy-duty high speed blender, measuring spoons and cups and pint size container with lid.

Raw is better kale salad

Servings:12. Preparation time: 40 minutes. Cooking time: 20 minutes. Total time: 60 minutes

Description: cheesy and delicious.

INGREDIENTS

1 bunch fresh curly leaf kale

1/4 pieces of red and yellow bell peppers 1/4 piece clean purple onion

1 tomato

1/2cup natural dried cherries

DIRECTIONS:

Wash well 1 bunch of fresh curly leaf kale and remove the stems (save the stems for a smoothie).

Cut kale in small pieces and drain.

Cut 2 small slices of red and yellow bell peppers into small pieces rinse

1 tomato chopped into small pieces

Put the kale bell peppers and tomatoes in a large bowl and massage well with hands, then put in salad spinner and spend out water and set aside.

Sauce:

2 tablespoons Bragg's apple cider vinegar

1 medium semi soft avocados

1 tablespoon grounded flaxseeds

1/4 cup walnut pieces

1/3 cup dried cherries soaked for 10 minutes in 1/3cup spring water. After soaking add the water and cherries to blender

1 tablespoon Bragg's liquid amino

1/8 teaspoon cayenne pepper optional

2 tablespoons cold pressed olive oil

3 tablespoons nutritional yeast

1/4cup of diaya cheddar cheese

Put the above items in blender and blend until creamy then add the last items and blend until creamy. Add the sauce to the kale and stir in well, making sure everything is mixed in well

Refrigerate to marinate overnight or for 20 minutes, and then enjoy!

Preparation items: large bowl. Sharp knife, large spoon, measuring spoons and cups, and cutting board and salad spinner

Raw smooth almond salad dressing

Yield:16 oz. Preparation Time: 3 minutes. Blending Time: 3 minutes. Total Time: 6 minutes

Description: With this recipe I had some raw almonds and decided to see if I could make a salad dressing with them so I put some almonds along with the base of my salad dressings and then I remembered that I had some poppy seeds and I use some and the end was a creamy salad dressing that can also be served as dip.

INGREDIENTS:

1/4cup sliced raw unsalted almonds

1/2cup extra virgin olive oil

1/4cup of Bragg's apple cider vinegar

3tablespoons agave nectar

1 cup almond milk

1/4teaspoon sea salt

2tablespoons grounded flaxseed

1-Small garlic clove peeled and rinsed

Small piece yellow onion peeled and rinsed

1 teaspoon poppy seeds

1 Pinch ground cayenne pepper

DIRECTIONS:

Put all of the ingredients in a heavy duty blender and blend on high speed until all ingredients are blended and dressing is smooth and creamy.

Taste and add more seasonings if needed.

Pour dressing into a medium container.

Rinse the blender with small amount milk and pour into the container.

Shake well before serving.

If the dressing is too thick add a little almond milk or spring water.

Preparation items: high speed blender, measuring cup and spoons and medium container.

Raw supreme carrot "mock tuna" salad

Serves: 12. Preparation Time: 20 minutes. Mixing Time: 10 minutes. Total Time: 30 minutes.

Description: I was looking for another way to use the pulp when I juiced carrots. So I tried mixing some seasoning added ground veggies to the carrot pulp and it turned out nice and very tasty so we use this recipe to make a quick meal on weekends. This raw carrot salad is so versatile. It can be placed on top of a tossed salad, placed on crackers as an appetizer or make a sandwich. It's awesome! We love it. The carrot juice is a refreshing and healthy drink.

INGREDIENTS:

20 fresh organic unpeeled carrots

1/4cup of fresh onions

1 fresh red bell

2 stalks of fresh celery

1 fresh clove garlic

2 tablespoons ground flaxseeds

1 teaspoon ground paprika

1/2 teaspoon cilantro

1/2 teaspoon kelp- optional

1/8 teaspoon cayenne pepper optional

3 tablespoons Bragg's liquid amino or to taste

3/4cup organic sweet pickle relish

2 tablespoons light agave nectar

1 quart Follow your heart vegenaise sandwich spread

1 teaspoon ground paprika

DIRECTIONS:

Peel the onion and garlic.

Put fresh cleaned onion, bell pepper, celery, and garlic in food processor and coarsely chop, then drained and set aside.

Drain relish and set aside.

Wash carrots well and remove blemishes and cut off ends.

Before juicing the carrots in juicer place the pulp catcher and the juice Catcher in place then began juicing.

In a large bowl empty the carrot pulp, the ground veggies and dry seasonings, flaxseeds and mix well.

Save the carrot juice to drink.

Add liquid amino, relish, agave nectar, sandwich spread and mix thoroughly.

Taste and add more seasoning and sandwich spread if needed.

Sprinkle a little paprika over the top of the carrot salad.

To make sandwich put some carrot salad on a slice of toasted bread and add leaves of romaine lettuce, alfalfa sprouts and tomato slices and add the other slice of toasted bread the on a slice of whole wheat bread and enjoy!

Preparation items: heavy duty juicer with pulp and juice catcher, large bowl, sharp knife, colander, measuring spoons and cups, cutting board, large spoon

Savory Garbanzo beans

Serve: 12. Preparation time: 10 minutes. Cook time: 55 minutes.
Total time: 1 hour + 5 minutes

Description: Very tasty and delicious and gluten free. Garbanzo beans
(also known as chickpeas, Bengal grams, and Egyptian peas) have a
delicious nutlike taste and buttery texture. These beans are very healthy
and versatile. I always cook up lots of beans and freeze them so I will
always have them on hand.

Remove blemished beans and rocks and soak the beans overnight in
spring water and aluminum -free baking soda.

Measure 3 cups and leftover beans can be frozen for using later.

Use 3cups presoaked garbanzo beans, rinsed well

1 small onion

3 cloves garlic

2 tablespoons olive oil

1 teaspoon grounded sage

1 teaspoon grounded ginger

1 teaspoon smoked paprika

1 tablespoon turmeric

1 teaspoon sea salt

1/4 teaspoon Cayenne pepper

1/2 red bell pepper washed and cubed

1 carrot ends cut off and wash and sliced

1 gallon spring water

Ground the onion and garlic very fine in the food processor and set aside.

Put the beans, grounded onions, garlic, oil and all dry ingredients in a large heavy duty pot and sauté for 5 minutes on top of the stove.

Then add enough water to cover the beans.

Start cooking on high heat to a boil, then turn heat to medium/low. Cover and simmer for 45 minutes or to desired tenderness.

Then add the carrots and red bell pepper and cook for about 10 minutes, until the veggies are tender.

Taste and add more seasons if needed. Serve with nutty flavored quinoa or long grain basmati brown rice.

Preparation item: heavy duty stainless steel pot with cover, large stirring spoon for Measuring spoons, measuring cup, cutting board, Knife and food processor

Savory lentil beans and mushroom

Serves: 8. Preparation Time: 8 minutes. Cooking Time: 33 minutes.
Total Time: 41 minutes.

Description: I love cooking these beans. They are very healthy and
quick to prepare and taste great with the mushrooms, any time of the
year.

INGREDIENTS:

3cups brown lentil beans - pick debris out and rinsed well

1/2 onion

2 large fresh tomatoes

3 garlic cloves

1 carrot

1 stalk celery

1 spring fresh rosemary

1 cup sliced mushrooms

1/8 teaspoon grounded cayenne pepper

1/2 teaspoon ground cumin

1/2 teaspoon ginger

1 teaspoon ground smoked paprika

1/4 teaspoon sea salt optional

3 tablespoons extra virgin olive oil

8 cups of spring water

DIRECTIONS:

Peel the onion and garlic and rinse all vegetables well and de-stem the rosemary.

Puree onions, rosemary leaves, celery, tomatoes and garlic in food processor.

Rinse the slice the mushrooms and carrot

Put the prepared lentils, seasonings, pureed veggies and all of the sliced veggies and olive oil in a large pot and sauté on medium heat on top of the stove for 3 minutes. Stir often so nothing burns or sticks to the pot.

Add the water and turn the heat to medium and cook for 25 minutes or until beans are tender.

Stir occasionally and add more water if needed.

For doneness, mash a bean between the fingers.

Stir and add the mushrooms and cook for 5 minutes.

Turn off the heat and serve warm.

Preparation items: medium heavy stainless steel pot with lid, measuring cups and spoons, stirring spoon, sharp knife, food processor and cutting board

Delicious spicy mushroom meat loaf

Serves:10. Preparation Time: 15 minutes. Cooking Time: 1hour 40 minutes. Total Time: 1hour 55 minutes. Soak protein overnight.

Description: Vegetable protein is very versatile and takes on the texture of what it is combined with. This meat loaf is savory and delicious. It also makes a beautiful showing. This meat loaf can be sliced and served with just mayo, sprouts and ketchup. Always soak enough for freezing

INGREDIENTS:

4cups of presoaked textured vegetable protein granules

1 large onion, peeled, rinsed and chopped

1 cup chopped mushrooms, rinsed and chopped

2 carrots peeled

4 cloves of garlic, peeled and rinsed

3 slices dairy- free spelt bread, toasted

1 cup raw cashews

2/3cup oat flour

2 tablespoons grounded flaxseeds

6 tablespoon spring water

1/4teaspoon red pepper seeds

3 teaspoons of smoked paprika

1 tablespoon grounded fennel

2 teaspoons fennel seeds

2 tablespoons ground sage

1/3 cup olive oil

1/4cup Bragg's liquid amino

1 cup daiya shredded vegan mozzarella cheese

1/4 cup diaya cheddar cheese

1 can organic non-stick olive oil spray

DIRECTIONS:

Preheat oven to 375 degrees

Spray baking dish with olive oil spray

Soak protein overnight in a bowl of spring water or soak for 30 minutes in bowl of boiling hot water. Squeeze the water out before using or freezing and measure out 4 cups.

Mix flaxseeds and 6 tablespoons water together to gel for 5 minutes.

Peel, rinse and chop garlic, onions and carrots in food processor.

Finely grind cashews in food processor.

Rinse and chop mushrooms

Finely grind spelt bread in food processor.

Put all of the above ingredients in a large bowl and mix well

Dump the protein mixture into prepared baking dish and shape with your hands into a loaf.

Bake covered for 1 hour.

Bake uncovered for 1/2 hour until top is firm.

Sprinkle shredded cheddar cheese over the top and put back in oven (uncovered) for about 10 minutes until cheese melts. Let loaf sit for 10 minutes on cooling board before serving.

Preparation items needed: Large baking dish with cover, sharp knife, measuring cups and spoons, cutting board, food processor and 2 large bowls.

Steamed okra & sautéed mushrooms

Serves: 4. Preparation Time: 5 minutes. Cooking Time: 20 minutes. Total Time: 25 minutes.

Description: Okra originated in the northeastern part of Africa (today it is known as Ethiopia). It is low in fat and is very healthy, along with mushrooms. My husband loves this recipe and I cook it often for him.

INGREDIENTS:

2 pounds of fresh okra

1/3 teaspoon onions powder

1/3 teaspoon garlic powder

1/8 teaspoon of sea salt

Pinch of cayenne pepper

1 package sliced mushrooms

+Use ingredient below with mushrooms

2 tablespoons earth balance spread

DIRECTIONS:

Cut off tops of the okra, rinse and drain and put in a medium size pot.

Add onions powder, garlic powder and salt and stir to mix everything together and steam on medium heat for 15 minutes.

Rinse, dry and slice the mushrooms.

In another stick- free pan, add all other ingredients and mushrooms and sauté for 3 minutes. Stir as needed.

Serve the sautéed mushrooms over the okra.

Preparation items needed: medium stainless steel pot, measuring cups and spoons, knife, bowl, cutting board and colander, large non-stick sauté pan, large plastic spoon.

Vegan mixed fruit pie

Serves: 12. Preparation Time: 15 minutes. Cooking Time: 45 minutes.
Total time: 1hr

Description: I like to experiment in the kitchen so I had a pear and
some Fuji apples and quince fruit and I wanted to make an apple desert;
I put them together and the result was delicious. Quince fruit is a fall
fruit.

INGREDIENTS:

1 pear

4 Fuji apples

2 quince fruits

1 teaspoon all spice

2 teaspoons grounded cinnamon

2 teaspoons organic alcohol-free vanilla flavor

1 tablespoon fresh lemon juice

1 cup pure maple syrup

1cup spring water

1 cup earth balance vegan margarine

1 tablespoon grounded flax seeds

2 tablespoons spring water

DIRECTIONS:

Preheat oven to 350 degrees.

Peel and core the apples, quince fruit and core the pear.

Mix flax seeds and water together and set aside.

Put the prepared fruit in a large bowl.

Mix in blender, the all spice, cinnamon, vanilla flavor, lemon juice, sweetener water, flax seed mixture and soft margarine together, then pour over the fruit and mix all ingredients together well.

Then pour mixture into a large oblong baking dish.

Sprinkle one and a half cups of crumb crust over the top of pie.

Crumb crust:

Bake in oven for 45 minutes or until fruit is tender and top is golden brown and juice is bubbling.

Cool before serving with vegan ice cream. Preparation items: large oven proof oblong baking dish, large mixing spoon, chopping board, wire rack, measuring cup and spoons

Beautiful carrot cream of wheat bread

Serves: 8. Preparation Time: 11 minutes. Cooking Time: 45 minutes. Total Time: 56 minutes

Description: I was juicing carrots to make carrot salad one day and I had about a cup full left. I thought, why not make cream of wheat bread with the juice and it turned out beautiful. Cream of wheat bread is light and easy to digest.

INGREDIENTS:

3 cups Nirav Soji farina cream of wheat

1/4 teaspoon real sea salt

2 teaspoons aluminum-free baking powder

1/2 teaspoon aluminum-free baking soda

1 cup fresh organic carrot juice

1 tablespoon light agave nectar

1/4 cup organic olive oil

2 tablespoons blond flaxseeds

6 tablespoons spring water

1-1/2cups almond milk

1 can organic non-stick olive oil spray

DIRECTIONS:

Preheat oven to 400 degrees

Spray 9 inch baking pan with organic non-stick olive oil spray.

Put the cream of wheat in a medium size bowl.

Add all dry ingredients and mix together well.

Add the carrot juice, agave nectar, olive oil, cup of the almond milk, flaxseed mixture and mix in well.

Let mixture sit for 5 minutes then whisk and add balance of milk. Whisk again to make sure the mixture consistency is loose and fluffy and everything is mixed in. Mix well. If the mixture is not loose and fluffy, add a little more almond milk.

Optional: raisins can be added

Pour into prepared baking pan and sprinkle 1 teaspoon of olive oil over the top.

Bake for 45 minutes until tooth pick comes out clean.

Tip: to soften the top of the bread, after baking cover with a lid.

Variety: 6-8 large muffins can be made with this recipe.

Preparation items: 9 inch baking pan, Measuring cups and spoons, whisker, non-stick large muffin pans and medium size bowl.

Delightful dirty couscous

Serves: 8. Preparation Time: 15 minutes. Cooking Time: 5 minutes.
Total Time: 20 minutes.

Description: couscous is a great dish that cooks up fluffy and delicious.
Couscous is very easy to cook. It is very versatile because it can be
used in many dishes. Couscous is pasta that can be used as a grain and
originated in northern Africa.

INGREDIENTS:

Cooking couscous:

1-1/3cups spring water

1 cup couscous

Let the water come to a boil on top of the stove then rinse the couscous
in a tiny holed strainer. Then put the couscous into the pot of hot water
and stir lightly. Cover and remove from the heat and leave the pot
covered for 7 minutes. Remove the lid and fluff up the couscous with a
fork.

Now it can be used in the manner desired.

Stir fry:

1/3 piece of green bell pepper washed and cubed

1/3 piece red onions peeled washed and cubed

1 carrot washed and sliced

1 ear of sweet corn washed with cob cut off

5 string beans washed, cut in small pieces

1 cabbage leaf washed and cut into small pieces

1/3 cup grape seed oil

1/8 teaspoon of cayenne pepper

1 teaspoon turmeric

2 tablespoons liquid amino or to taste

1/8 teaspoon of cilantro

1/8 teaspoon grounded paprika

DIRECTIONS:

Put all washed and prepared vegetables in a large non-stick sauté pan.

Add the oil, pepper and turmeric to the pan and sauté on top of the stove for 3 minutes.

Remove from the heat and add the cooked couscous, liquid amino and fluff everything together. Sprinkle the cilantro and paprika on top.

Serve warm.

Preparation items: measuring cup, large heavy stainless steel sauté pan, large stirring spoon and fork, knife and cutting board.

Note: If serving couscous as a side dish, add 1 tablespoon of liquid amino and 1 tablespoon of olive oil or earth balance margarine to the water before boiling.

Vegan oatmeal raisin cookies

Yields: 30 medium cookies.   Preparation Time: 10 minutes.   Cooking
Time: 12 minutes per batch.   Total Time: 50 minutes.

Description: Memories of homemade oatmeal cookies are on my mind,
so I decided to make vegan style oatmeal raisin cookies. These cookies
are made with lot of oats, raisins, seeds and nuts. They are delicious
and healthy and not overly sweet.

INGREDIENTS:

2 cups of spelt flour

1/2teaspoon aluminum free baking powder

1/2 teaspoon aluminum free baking soda

1/4 teaspoon sea salt optional

2 teaspoon cinnamon

2 cups rolled gluten free oatmeal

2 tablespoon grounded flax seeds mixed in 6 tablespoons spring water

2 tablespoons chopped raw sunflower seeds

2/3 cup maple syrup

1/3 cup vegan raw sugar

1/2 cup extra virgin olive oil

2 teaspoons alcohol free real vanilla flavor

1 cup chopped walnuts

1/2cup organic raisins

Parchment paper

1 can organic non-stick olive oil spray

DIRECTIONS:

Preheated oven to 375

Cover cookie sheet with parchment paper and spray lightly.

Chop walnuts and sunflower seeds in food processor and set aside.

Put the flour, oats, sea salt, baking soda, baking powder, cinnamon, chopped sunflower seeds and walnuts in a bowl and stir well.

Put olive oil, flavor, maple syrup, sugar, flaxseed mixture in blender and blend well.

Then add the wet mixture to the flour mixture and mix with a large spoon until everything is moist and mixed well.

Spray small cookie scooper or small ice-cream scooper with non-stick spray and dip up the cookie dough and drop the dough onto the cookie sheet and press lightly with plastic cup sprayed with non-stick spray. Continue the process until all cookies are cooked and spaced apart.

Bake 10 minutes.

Let cookies cool for 5 minutes then remove from the parchment paper.

Use wax paper between each layer of cookies to prevent them from sticking together when placing in a container.

Note: 1-1/2cups turbinino sugar in the raw and 1/2 cup almond milk can be used for sweetener instead of maple syrup.

Preparation items: large bowl, parchment paper, measuring cups and spoons, blender, medium cookie dough scooper or ice-cream scooper, plastic cup, spatula, tablespoon, wax paper and food processor.

Garbanzo beans Meat-less chili

Serves: 20.   Preparation Time: 1 hour + 40 minutes.   Cooking Time: 1 hour + 40 minutes.   Total Time: 1hour + 50 minutes

Description: This is very tasty and it's full of healthy veggies. The preparation time is a little long but the result is a delicious chili, made from scratch.

*This chili can be frozen for later use.

INGREDIENTS:

1/3 cup extra virgin olive oil

4 large Roma tomatoes rinsed grounded

1 large carrot washed and grounded

6 cloves of garlic peeled rinsed

1 large onions peeled and rinsed

2 cups presoaked garbanzo beans

2 cups presoaked textured vegetable protein granules

3 tablespoons cumin, grounded

1/2 small Scot bonnet pepper add more if desired

2 tablespoons whole dried basil flakes

1 tablespoon dried oregano flakes

3 tablespoons paprika powder

6 tablespoon chili powder

3 tablespoons Bragg's liquid amino

1 teaspoon grounded ginger

24 ounce jar rega gluten free organic Italian tomato puree

1 can Woodstock gluten free organic tomato Paste

2 tablespoons Canadian pure maple syrup add last

1 fresh red bell peppers cored rinsed add last

1 fresh green bell pepper, cored and rinsed add last

1 teaspoon aluminum free baking soda only if soaking beans overnight

1 gallon spring water

DIRECTIONS:

Soak protein granules for 30 minutes in boiling hot water in a large bowl or soak overnight. Squeeze out the water before using in a recipe or freezing. Measure out 2 cups for recipe.

Pick out any small stones from the beans.

Soak beans overnight in one teaspoon aluminum-free baking soda and enough water to cover them or follow directions on bag for quick soaking, but omit baking soda. After soaking the beans rinse well. Drain the beans and measure out 2 cups in a large pot.

Grind tomatoes fine in food processor before adding to the chili pot.

Put carrot, Scot bonnet pepper and garlic in food processor and grind very fine.

Chop onion in small pieces in food processor.

Put the olive oil, presoaked vegetable protein, seasonings, prepared onions, prepared garlic, Scot bonnet pepper and carrot into the pot.

Put the pot on top of the stove and sauté for 5 minutes and stir often.

Add 4 cups water, liquid amino, grounded tomatoes to the pot and gently mix thoroughly.

Start the cooking process on high heat, uncovered until the chili bean began to boil, then turn heat to medium/low covered and cook for 60 minutes or until beans are tender. Add water if needed.

Stir the chili often to keep it from sticking.

Add last 2 cups of water and tomato puree, tomato paste, sweetener, chopped bell peppers and simmer on low heat for 35 minutes. Taste and add more seasonings if needed. Garnish with green onions; this is optional.

Preparation items: Large heavy duty stainless steel pot with cover, large stirring spoon for Measuring spoons, measuring cup, cutting board, knife and food processor.

Grilled barbeque tofu steak

Serves: 12. Preparation Time: 30 minutes. Cooking time: 42 minutes
Total time: 1hour+12 minutes

INGREDIENTS:

2 packs extra firm organic sprouted tofu

1/2 cup Bragg's liquid amino

1 teaspoon grounded turmeric

1/2 onion peeled, washed and sliced thin

1 teaspoon onion powder

1 teaspoon garlic powder

1 tablespoon smoked paprika

1 tablespoon nutritional yeast

1/2cup olive oil

1/2 teaspoon of cayenne pepper

1 tablespoon Bragg's apple cider vinegar

DIRECTIONS:

Preheat indoor pancake grill to 375 degrees, preheat oven to 400 degree. Spread the barbeque sauce over the bottom of the baking pan and set aside. Sauté onions and set aside

Homemade orange barbeque sauce page 33

Rinse and dry tofu well, then slice the tofu into 6 medium slices for each package. Makes about 12 slices and 24 pieces if cut in half.

Put all dry ingredients, liquid amino, half of the oil and vinegar in a small cup and stir well. Spread the mixture over the sliced tofu and let marinate for 30 minutes. Then place six pieces of the sliced tofu or 12 pieces if cut in half on the indoor grill and sprinkle some of the reserve oil over the tofu and cook the tofu steaks until they are brown about 4 minutes.

Then turn over and spread the remaining seasoning and oil over the tops of the steaks and continue cooking about 4 minutes on each side, until brown. Continue until all of tofu is cooked and browned well.

Remove tofu from the grill and place in the stainless steel pan and spread barbecue sauce and 2 tablespoons of olive oil over the tofu and cook in oven on 400 degrees, uncovered for 25 minutes.

Optional: spread sautéed onions on the top of the baked tofu. Serve warm as a meat substitute.

Preparation items: indoor pancake grill, knife, measuring cups and spoons, cutting board, non-stick sauté pan, medium cup, large stainless steel baking pan.

Hearty angel hair nests vegetable soup

Serves: 8. Preparation time: 10 minutes. Cooking time: 55 minutes.
Total time: 1 hour + 5 minutes

Description: This soup is good anytime but we like this soup in the
winter; it is hearty and warms you up. It has lots of veggies.

INGREDIENTS:

4 tablespoons Bragg's liquid amino

1 teaspoon ground paprika

Dash of cayenne pepper or to taste

1 teaspoon basil flakes

1 medium piece of fresh rosemary

1/2 teaspoon grounded turmeric

2 tablespoons grape seed oil

2 tomatoes

3 garlic cloves

1 small onion

1/2 teaspoon pure maple syrup add last

2 each fresh kale leaves purple and green leave

2 turnip roots

1 ear of corn

1 carrot

8 cups spring water

2 rice angel hair nests coils of pasta

DIRECTIONS:

Wash and rinse the vegetable and rosemary and set aside.

Peel, rinse and take all of the silk off the corn, then cut the corn off the cob and set aside.

Peel and rinse the onion and garlic.

Put the onion, garlic, rosemary leaves and prepared tomatoes in a food processor and chop well.

Rinse and slice the carrot.

Slice the prepared kale in thin slices.

Wash and cut turnip root into small cubes.

Add the oil, kale, turnip roots, carrots, grounded onions, garlic, tomatoes, rosemary leaves and seasonings in the pot and sauté for 5 minutes on top of the stove on medium low heat.

Put 8 cups of water in the pot and stir and let soup come to a boil then reduce the heat to medium and cook covered for 35 minutes

Add the prepared corn stir and simmer on low heat covered for 10 minutes or until turnip root is tender.

Taste and add maple syrup and more seasoning if needed.

Stir in angel hair nest spaghetti and turn off heat.

Variety: 1/2 cup presoaked mock beef chips can be added during the cooking process but soak mock beef chips for 30 minutes in boiling hot water in a bowl and rinse the chips well and squeeze out the water before using in recipe.

Serve hot.

Preparation items: cutting board, large stainless steel pot with lid, food processor, sharp knife, large stirring spoon, soup dipper, bowl, measuring cups and spoons.

Quick savory tomato gravy

Yield: 2 cups. Preparation Time: 8 minutes. Cooking Time:16 minutes. Total Time: 24 minutes

Description: I was looking for gravy for mashed potato, so I decided to make gravy with ketchup and add some roma tomatoes, spices and the gravy turned out great; it's quick, easy and tasty.

INGREDIENTS:

3 tablespoons extra virgin olive oil

1 medium onion peeled rinsed and sliced

2 garlic cloves peeled rinsed chopped

2 Roma tomatoes rinsed chopped

1 cup organic fructose and gluten free tomato ketchup

3 cups spring water mixed with 1 tablespoon potato starch

1 tablespoon pure maple syrup

2 tablespoons Bragg's liquid amino

1 teaspoon grounded paprika

1/3 teaspoon basil flakes

1/8 teaspoon ground cayenne pepper

DIRECTIONS:

Chop onions and garlic in food processor

Chopped tomatoes

Sauté onions and garlic in olive oil for 1 minute, then add the chopped tomatoes, ketchup, water and starch mixture, liquid amino, maple syrup, paprika, basil and cayenne pepper. Stir and cook for 15 minutes or until the gravy becomes thickened. A little water can be added if the gravy is too thick.

Preparation items: large heavy duty stainless steel fry pan, medium bowl, fork, measuring cup and spoons, large stirring spoon.

Apple and pineapple compote

Serves: 5. Preparation Time: 10 minutes. Cooking Time: 35minutes
Total Time: 45 minutes

Description: I mixed fresh pineapples with the Fuji apples and this combination is simply beautiful and enjoyable.

INGREDIENTS:

6 Fuji organic apples, unpeeled, washed, sliced in medium wedges and cored

1/2 cup cubed fresh pineapples

4 tablespoons of maple syrup

4 teaspoons earth balance original spread or margarine

1 teaspoon vanilla

1-1/2 teaspoons cinnamon

1/2 teaspoon all spice

DIRECTIONS:

74

Peel pineapple or buy one already peeled and reserve 1/2 cup.

Put the prepared apples in a medium pot on top of the stove.

Add all of the seasonings and stir well.

Cook apples for 25 minutes then add the pineapple and stir and cook for another 10 minutes.

Serve alone as a desert.

For variety, add a scoop of coconut milk vanilla bean ice cream on top.

Preparation items: medium heavy duty stainless steel pot with lid, stirring spoon, measuring spoons and cup, cutting board and knife

Avocado dip

Serves: 20. Preparation Time: 6 minutes. Mixing Time: 10 minutes. Total Time: 16 minutes.

Description: Creamy with a hint of lemon and is gluten free

INGREDIENTS:

4 medium ripe organic avocados rinsed, dried and peeled with seed and peels discarded.

1/2 small purple onion peeled, rinsed and chopped fine

3 tablespoons lemon juice

1 small garlic clove peeled, rinsed and chopped fine

1/4 Piece red bell pepper chopped

1/8 teaspoon cayenne pepper

1/8 teaspoon basil

1/8 teaspoon real sea salt

DIRECTIONS:

Chop all the vegetables in food processor real fine and set aside.

Put the avocados in a food processor and chop. Transfer the chopped avocados to a medium bowl and add the chopped veggies, seasonings and stir well to blend everything together.

Transfer the dip to a pretty bowl and serve immediately or cover and refrigerate.

Serve on your favorite crackers, blue chips and or celery sticks.

Preparation items: food processor, measuring cup and spoons, medium bowl, knife, cutting bowl, serving spoon and pretty bowl.

Awesome carrot "tuna" salad & pasta

Serves: 15. Preparation Time: 25 minutes. Mixing Time: 18 minutes. Total Time: 43 minutes.

Description: This recipe is awesome and quick. Excellent and simply delicious with a tossed salad

INGREDIENTS:

20 fresh organic unpeeled carrots, washed with ends cut off and dried

1/2 of fresh purple onion peeled and rinsed

3 fresh cloves garlic peeled and rinsed

1 small fresh red bell pepper rinsed and cored

2 stalks of celery rinsed and sliced

2 tablespoons ground flax seeds

1 teaspoon ground paprika

1/8 teaspoon cayenne pepper

1/3 cup Bragg's liquid amino

1/2 teaspoon grounded kelp optional

1 cup drained organic sweet relish before adding to salad

2 tablespoons light agave nectar

3 cups of follow your heart vegenaise sandwich spread, add more if needed.

1-12 ounce box fusillin pasta

2 sprigs fresh parsley

1 organic cucumber

DIRECTIONS:

Boil pasta according to the directions on the box. Rinse pasta with cold spring water and set aside.

Put onion, garlic, bell pepper and celery in food processor and ground very fine, then drain and set aside.

Before juicing the carrots in juicer, place the pulp catcher and the juice catcher in place and began juicing. Reserve left over juice to drink

When finished, put the carrot pulp, the ground veggies, dry seasonings in a large bowl and mix well.

Add liquid amino, paprika, relish, agave nectar, sandwich spread and mix thoroughly.

Taste and add more seasoning if needed. Add 2 cups of the carrot salad

To the prepared pasta and mix well. Cover leftover carrot salad and refrigerate.

Sprinkle ground paprika over the top of the salad and decorate with fresh parsley and sliced fresh cucumbers around the sides. Refrigerate for 1 hour before serving.

Preparation items: heavy duty juicer with pulp and juice catcher, large bowl, knife, colander, measuring spoons and cups, cutting board, large spoon

Baked almond tofu steaks

Serves: 9. Preparation Time: 15 minutes. Cook time: 40 minutes. Total time: 55 minutes.

Description: These slices of tofu are crunchy and light and prefect for a meat substitute or a sandwich.

INGREDIENTS:

Preheat oven to 375 degrees

1-1/2packs extra firm organic sprouted tofu rinsed

1 cup raw creamy almond salad dressing

1 tablespoon turmeric powder

1 tablespoon smoked paprika powder

1/2teaspoon Garlic powder

1/2 teaspoon onion Powder

1/8 teaspoon of cayenne pepper

3 tablespoons Bragg's liquid amino

1 tablespoon extra-virgin olive oil

1 can organic non-stick olive oil spray

1-1/2cups almonds

DIRECTIONS:

Slice tofu into medium thick slices, about 6 slices out of the pack and 3 slices out of the half.

Put the almonds and cayenne pepper, paprika, turmeric in the food processor and ground very fine then set aside.

Mix the salad dressing, liquid amino, garlic and onion powder together in bowl.

Put the sliced tofu in a plate and pour the salad dressing mixture on top and marinate for 10 minutes.

Coat the wet sliced tofu with the grounded almond mixture on both sides.

Place the coated tofu on parchment paper and sprinkle tops with olive oil.

Sprinkle leftover almond mixture on top of the tofu and bake 40 minutes in oven until slices are brown.

Serve warm.

Preparation items: cutting board, knife, large baking pan, parchment paper, measuring spoons and cup, 1 large plates, food processor, small bowl

Baked spicy and cheesy potatoes

Serves: 12. Preparation Time: 10 minutes. Cooking Time: 50 minutes. Total Time: 60 minutes

Description: These potato wedges are very cheesy and go well as a side dish with any meal or eat alone as an appetizer.

INGREDIENTS:

Preheat oven to 375

6 large red potatoes

1 package grated daiya dairy free yellow cheese

1/4 teaspoon sea salt

1/2 teaspoon of cayenne pepper

1 teaspoon grounded paprika

1 teaspoon grounded turmeric

1/3 teaspoon garlic powder

1/2 teaspoon onion powder

1 can organic non-stick olive oil spray

Parchment paper

Aluminum foil

DIRECTIONS:

Spray baking pan with olive oil spray and set aside.

Washed the potatoes with skin on and cut them in medium wedges

Place all of the seasonings in a gallon size bag. Then add the potato wedges and shake well. Let the potato wedges sit in the bag with the seasoning for 5 minutes.

Place the prepared wedges in the prepared baking pan.

Bake covered with parchment paper with aluminum foil on top of parchment paper for about 35 minutes.

Then take out of the oven and sprinkle grated cheese generously over the top.

Leave pan uncovered and put back into the oven until the cheese melts about 15 minutes. Serve hot plain or with sour cream, mustard and ketchup.

Preparation items: medium baking pan, measuring spoons and cup, sharp knife, gallon size plastic bag, cutting board and toothpicks.

Spicy baked barbeque tofu steaks

Serves: 12. Preparation Time: 10 minutes. Cooking Time: 60 minutes. Total Time: 1 hour + 10 minutes

Description: spicy tofu and wonderful barbeque sauce

INGREDIENTS:

2 packs extra organic firm tofu

3 tablespoons Bragg's liquid amino

1 teaspoon grounded turmeric

2 stalks fresh green onions

1 teaspoon onion powder

1 teaspoon garlic powder

2 teaspoons smoked paprika

1/3cup cold pressed olive oil

1/8 teaspoon of cayenne pepper

Homemade orange barbeque sauce, p.33

DIRECTIONS:

Preheat oven to 400 degrees

Spread the barbeque sauce over the bottom of the baking pan and set aside

Sauté the green onions in one teaspoon oil and set aside

Slice the tofu into medium slices. Makes about 6 medium slices each pack or cut the slices in half and make 24 pieces

Put all of dry ingredients, oil and liquid amino in a cup and stir well. Now spread some of the mixture over the sliced tofu. Put the tofu in the oven and bake the tofu steaks until they are well browned about 20 minutes before turning over.

Then turn over and spread some of the mixture over the tops of the steaks and continue to cook for about 20 minutes, until that side is well brown.

Remove from the oven and spread barbeque sauce on the top of the tofu. Continue to bake in the oven 15 minutes then spread sautéed onions on top. Serve hot as a meat substitute.

Variety: Grated parmesan cheese can be sprinkled generously on top.

Preparation items: knife, measuring cups and spoons, sauté pan, cutting board, 1 large stainless steel baking pan, medium cup.

Basic walnut crumb crust

Yield: One 9 inch pie or one oblong pie. Preparation Time: 10 minutes.
Mixing time: 15 minutes. Total time:25 minutes.

Description: This recipe can be modified with different spices to
complement the recipe that is being used.

INGREDIENTS:

1 cup spelt flour

1/2 cup walnuts

1 1/2 sticks cold earth balance buttery spread sliced

1/4 teaspoon sea salt

3 tablespoons organic raw brown sugar

Squeeze out 1tablespoon fresh lemon juice from a lemon

DIRECTIONS:

Grind the walnuts very fine and add to dry ingredients. Then put all dry ingredients, margarine slices and lemon juice in a bowl or food processor.

Chop with a pastry cutter until all ingredients are mixed well together and crumbly.

Put into a pie dish and pat out with your hands until you have a pie crust or crumb crust can be sprinkled on top of a fruit pie before baking or any recipe that calls for a crumb crust.

Preparation items: food processor, lemon squeezer, measuring cup and spoons, food processor, knife, pastry cutter, fork and pie pan

Basil steamed cabbage

Serves: 8. Preparation time: 10 minutes. Cooking Time: 15 minutes. Total Time: 25 minutes

Description: I love cabbage! It's healthy and has lots of vitamins. I don't overcook it, the southern traditional way. I cook the cabbage until crunchy

INGREDIENTS:

1 medium fresh cabbage sliced thin

1 small fresh onion peeled rinsed and sliced

1 yellow bell pepper rinsed and sliced thin

3 tablespoons organic extra-virgin olive oil (add last)

1/4teaspoon sea salt

1/8teaspoon basil flakes

Pinch cayenne pepper

DIRECTIONS:

Slice cabbage and veggies thinly.

Wash the onion and cabbage in a large basin or in a clean sink and drain in colander before putting the cabbage in a large pot.

Add all of the dry seasoning, half cup spring water and stir to mix the seasoning and cabbage together and cover.

Let the cabbage come to a quick steam on high heat on top of the stove then turn heat to low and steam covered for 15 minutes.

Taste and add oil, stir and add more seasoning if needed.

Turn off the heat and leave the pot on burner.

Serve hot.

Variety: 1/2 teaspoon of turmeric and a few raisins can be stirred into the cabbage.

Preparation items: large heavy duty pot with lid, large basin, chopping board, measuring cups and spoons, stirring spoon, knife and colander

Best Sesame spinach ever

Serves: 6. Preparation Time: 18 minutes. Cooking Time: 3 minutes.
Total Time: 21 minutes.

Description: Colorful and taste great!

INGREDIENTS:

3 bunches of fresh spinach

1 tablespoon sesame seeds

1 tablespoon grape seed oil

1/4 teaspoon real sea salt

1 pinch cayenne pepper more if desired

1 teaspoon garlic powder

1 teaspoon Aluminum-free baking soda

DIRECTIONS:

Soak spinach 10 minutes in baking soda and water to remove dirt.

Then rewash the spinach 2 times in water or until clean.

Drain and put the spinach in a salad spinner to remove all of the water

Put the spinach in a medium pot and add the dry seasonings, cover pot and let come to a boil about 1minute on medium high heat on top of the stove. Then stir to mix the seasonings and spinach together

Turn heat to low and steam the spinach covered for 3 minutes.

Drain any liquid and save for stock later.

Pour the grape seed oil over and stir the spinach well. Then sprinkle sesame seeds over spinach.

Remove from the heat and serve as a side dish

Preparation items: medium size stainless steel pot colander, measuring spoons and cups, salad spinner and knife.

Blueberry basic cake with blueberry drizzle frosting

Serves: 12. Preparation Time: 15 minutes. Cooking Time: 45 minutes. Total Time: 1 hour

Description: I like this basic cake because I can add what I want to it or use as a plain cake. In this picture I used blueberries for the fruit and made a blueberry icing.

INGREDIENTS:

Can of non-stick organic olive oil spray

3-1/2 cups basic cake flour-recipe

2 teaspoons aluminum-free baking powder

1 teaspoon aluminum-free baking soda

1/4teaspoon real sea salt

1 cup soft soy free earth balance spread

1/3 cup grape seed oil

2 tablespoons light grounded flaxseeds mixed with 6 tablespoons warm spring water

3/4cup almond milk or juice from fruit

1 cup Easy homemade unsweetened applesauce page 15

2 teaspoons vanilla flavor

2 cups raw organic light brown cane sugar

Can organic olive oil non-stick spray

DIRECTIONS:

Preheat oven to 350 degrees.

Spray a bundt pan well with non-stick olive oil spray and sprinkle the pan lightly with flour and shake out excess and set aside.

Sift the cake flour, baking powder, baking soda and salt into a large bowl.

In the food processor, mix the earth balance spread, oil, milk, raw sugar, vanilla flavor, flaxseed mixture and applesauce together until creamy.

Add the wet mixture to the flour mixture mixing well after each addition.

Continue using all of the wet mixture and mix well.

Scrape the sides of bowl and continue to mix just enough to blend everything together with electric mixer about 30 seconds.

++If adding cooked fresh fruit drain the fruit and nuts

Pour half of the cake mixture into the prepared pan and shake the pan to even out the cake mixture then add the well-drained fruit and finely chopped nuts.

Then pour the balance of the cake mix into the pan and shake to even out the mixture in the pan.

Bake for 55 minutes then inserted long wooden skewer in center to see if comes out clean. If uncooked batter or crumbs is on tooth pick cook 3-4 minutes and test again.

After 10 minutes, remove cake out of cake pan to a plate to cool completely before frosting.

*Frosting of your choice or blueberry drizzle frosting page 92

Preparation items: large non-stick bundt pan, measuring cups and spoons, whisker, electric mixer, large spoon, knife, large bowl and cutting board.

Blueberry drizzle frosting

Yield: 1 cup.   Preparation Time: 10 minutes.
Cooking Time: 5 minutes.   Total Time: 15 minutes.

Description: This drizzle frosting is colorful, delicious and versatile. Can be used on pancakes or waffles with fresh blue berries on top.

INGREDIENTS:

3 cups vegan raw brown sugar

3 tablespoons unbleached flour

2 tablespoons almond milk

3 tablespoons soft earth balance spread

1 teaspoon alcohol free vanilla flavor

1/2 cup fresh blueberries

DIRECTIONS:

Powder the brown sugar in a heavy duty blender on high speed and set aside.

Bring the milk and blueberries to a boil in a pot on top of the stove for about one minute, then remove pot and mash the blueberries with a fork and set aside.

Put the earth balance spread and flour in a medium pot on top of the stove on low heat and continuously whisk with a whisker for 1 minute or until the earth balance and flour is blended together.

Add the blue berries mixture and whisk briskly to mix everything together. Let cool completely.

When mixture is cooled, beat with the electric mixer on medium speed. Adding the prepared sugar and flavor, continue beating on low speed until smooth.

Makes enough to dribble down the sides and cover the top of one cake. Decorate with fresh blue berries.

Preparation items: 2 medium stainless pots, measuring cup and spoons, medium bowl, whisker and electric mixer, heavy duty blender.

Breakfast scrambled or cubed tofu

Serves: 3.   Preparation Time: 3 minutes.
Cooking Time: 10 minutes.   Total Time: 13 minutes.

Description: Colorful and taste great. Good low fat substitute for scrambled eggs

For variety, I like to add shredded vegan cheese when the tofu is cooked and still hot.

Any vegetables can be added to the tofu while cooking.

*This dish can be used to make scrambled tofu sandwiches: I use whole wheat pita bread or gluten free sliced bread and spread the bread with vegan sandwich spread. Then put shredded lettuce, tofu, alfalfa sprouts and chopped tomatoes on the sandwich. Also I use this dish as a side dish along with grits, toast or waffles,

INGREDIENTS:

2 tablespoons extra virgin olive oil (water can be used instead of oil if preferred)

1 1/2Packs firm organic tofu rinsed dried and crumbled

1/2 fresh purple onions-optional

1/3 piece red bell pepper-optional

1/8 teaspoon cayenne pepper

1/2 teaspoon grounded turmeric

1-1/2 tablespoons Bragg's liquid amino

DIRECTIONS:

Peeled rinsed the onion and chopped thin

Rinse the bell pepper and slice thin.

Put a large non-stick sauté pan on top of the stove and turn the heat to medium.

Crumble tofu into the sauté pan and add the sliced veggies and all of the dry seasonings and flip over with a plastic pancake flipper to mix in the seasonings and veggies and let the tofu mixture start to cook.

Add the olive oil, liquid amino to the pan and stir.

Cook on medium heat for 10 minutes, flipping the tofu over at intervals.

Taste, add more seasoning if needed. Serve hot.

Preparation items: paring knife, large heavy non-stick sauté pan measuring cup and spoons, cutting board and plastic pancake flipper.

Broccoli and pasta with gold sauce

Serves: 6.   Preparation Time: 10 minutes.   Cooking Time: 20 minutes.   Total Time: 30 minutes.

Description: This dish is colorful and quick to cook.

I like to use brown rice gluten free pasta; it's light and healthy.

INGREDIENTS:

1 Large head of fresh broccoli

1/3 piece of red bell pepper, rinsed and cubed

1/2 teaspoon garlic powder

1/2 teaspoon onion powder

2 teaspoons organic extra virgin oil

1/3 cup spring water

1/2 box brown rice gluten free pasta

1/2 cup daiya cheddar style shredded cheese.

DIRECTIONS:

Cook the pasta according to directions on the box. Then drain and rinse under cold water and set aside.

Gold sauce recipe on page 31 make ahead of time and set aside

Cut the hard stalks off the broccoli and peel them. Then cut the broccoli into medium pieces and wash well..

Put the broccoli, water, seasonings and red bell peppers in medium pot with cover and bring to a boil. Then turn off the heat and keep covered and steam for 8 minutes on top of the stove.

Add the cooked pasta, gold sauce and stir and remove from the burner.

Serve warm as a side dish.

If desired sprinkle with dairy free daiya cheddar style shredded cheese on top

Preparation items: large stainless steel pot, measuring cup and spoons, knife, colander and cutting board

Caribbean style pigeon peas and rice

Serves: 8. Preparation Time: 8 minutes. Cooking Time: 1 hrs +30 minutes. Total time1hr+ 38 minutes

Description: I call the liquid from the peas "pot liker" because it brings back memories from my southern roots. Pigeon pea, also called the Congo or Gunga pea, they have a nutty taste.

This recipe was introduced to me from an old friend from the Caribbean.

INGREDIENTS:

2 cups long grain basmati brown rice

2 cups presoaked pigeon peas

1/2 onion washed, peeled

1 teaspoon ground ginger

1/2 teaspoon ground thyme

2 fresh garlic cloves peeled rinsed

Small slice of scoot bonnet hot pepper; use sparingly this pepper is very hot!

1/2 teaspoon real sea salt

1/2 of red bell peppers cored rinsed and chopped in food processor

3 cups spring water

1 teaspoon aluminum-free baking powder for soaking peas

Add these ingredients when peas are done:

Add 2 cups organic coconut milk

Olive oil

2 cups hot pot liker

DIRECTIONS:

Soaking the peas:

First, pick out any small rocks or debris then soak in spring water and

1 teaspoon aluminum-free baking soda overnight then drain and rinse well.

These peas can be soaked ahead of time and frozen until needed.

Soak the rice for 6 minutes then rinse and set aside.

Chop the vegetables in a food processor very fine.

Put the presoaked peas in a large pot on top of the stove and add the prepared veggies, seasonings and 3 cups of water and bring the pot to a boil. Reduce heat to medium and cook for 1 hour or until peas are fully cooked and tender. Add water if needed.

Drain off the pot liker and keep hot in a small pot. Unused peas and pot liker can be frozen for soup.

Add the hot pot liker, coconut milk, oil to the pot and stir lightly and bring to a boil. Reduce heat to medium/low and add the prepared rice, and cook covered for 30 minutes or until rice is tender and the liquid is absorbed. Add small amounts of the pot liker to the pot if needed, if rice is not tender. Turn off burner and leave pot covered for 4 minutes.

Fluff the peas and rice before serving.

Preparation items: large heavy bottom stainless steel pot with lid, measuring spoons and cups, food processor, large colander, large bowl and sharp knife

Chick-less flavored tofu strips

Serves: 8. Preparation Time: 15 minutes. Cooking Time: 25 minutes Total Time: 40 minutes

Description: These strips make a good appetizer before the main meal.

Serve hot with ketchup, Dijon mustard or hot sauce on the side.

INGREDIENTS:

2 blocks of extra firm organic sprouted tofu cut in medium strips

2 tablespoons grounded poultry seasoning

1 teaspoon garlic powder

1 teaspoon onion powder

1 teaspoon smoked paprika

2 teaspoons grounded turmeric

1/4 teaspoon cayenne pepper

1/2 cup of Bragg's liquid amino

2/3 cup light olive oil use half on each batch of tofu strips

1 large plastic bag

DIRECTIONS:

Thoroughly mix all dry ingredients together and set aside.

Put the strips on a large bowl and pour the liquid amino over the strips and let sit for 5 minutes.

Put half of the prepared dry ingredients into a large plastic bag.

Add 1/2 half of the tofu strips to the bag and gently shake to coat the strips.

Heat half of oil in a large heavy fry pan.

Fry the first batch of strips on medium heat on top of the stove for 3 minutes on each side until brown. After browning, place the strips in a plate on top of paper towels.

Continue the process until all of the strips are cooked then clean the frying pan and put all of the strips back to the frying pan and pour the leftover liquid amino over the strips and toss gently and leave the strips on the burner until liquid amino is absorbed. Then turn off the heat. Remove from pan to a large plate covered with white paper towels.

Serve hot at once with ketchup, Dijon mustard or hot sauce on the side.

Preparation items: large heavy duty frying pan, measuring cups and spoons, 2 large bowls, 2 large plate, fork, knife, plastic bag, cutting board and pancake flipper and paper towels.

Chocolate strawberry frosting

Yield: Frost 1 cake.   Preparation Time: 5 minutes.
Blending time: 5 minutes.   Total time: 10 minutes.

Description: Rich and creamy and very easy to prepare and is so delicious.

INGREDIENTS:

1/8 cup of earth balance spread

1/8 cup earth balance shortening

1/2 cup of unsweetened cocoa

4 cups organic confection sugar sifted

1 pinch aluminum free baking soda

1 teaspoon alcohol free strawberry or vanilla flavor

3 fresh strawberries washed well and topped

DIRECTIONS:

Put the earth balance and shortening in a small pot on top of the stove to melt.

Add the cocoa and stir to mix.

Remove from heat and stir.

Add the sifted confection sugar, pinch baking soda and flavor and mix with a spoon until incorporated, then with electric mixer for about 1 minute.

If the frosting is too thick, add a little almond milk until you reach the consistency desired.

Frost completely cooled cake and top with sliced strawberries.

Preparation items: medium stainless steel pot, measuring cups and spoons, electric mixer, knife and stirring spoon.

Cooked long grain basmati brown rice

Serves: 10.   Preparation Time: 8 minutes. Cooking Time: 30 minutes.
Total Time: 38 minutes.

Description: This was a difficult rice to cook and it took a lot of
experimenting to get it right. Basmati rice is grown in the Himalayas
and Pakistan and has a nutty flavor. This rice cooks up real fluffy and
tastes great.

INGREDIENTS:

2 cups Basmati long grain brown rice rinsed well

2 tablespoons earth balance buttery spread

4 cups spring water

1/4teaspoon sea salt- optional

6 whole cloves

DIRECTIONS:

Put the rice into a small holed strainer and rinse well and drain.

In a medium pot, add 4 cups of water and let the rice sit in the water for 6 minutes. Soaking make the rice easier to cook.

After soaking, add the earth balance spread, cloves and salt. Bring the rice to a boil on top of the stove takes about 4 minutes to boil.

Turn the heat to medium/ low and let the rice cook for 30 minutes in a tightly covered pot. Do not stir during this process and do not open the pot.

Watch the rice carefully and after 30 minutes, mash a grain of rice to test for doneness. If the rice is not done, add 1/8 cup of water. Turn off the heat and leave pot on the burner and keep covered and wait 4 more minutes, then fluff the rice with a fork and serve.

Preparation items: medium size heavy bottom stainless steel pot with lid, small holed strainer, measuring cups and spoons.

Vegan cream cheese frosting

Yield: Frost one cake.   Preparation Time: 5 minutes.   Blending time: 5 minutes.   Total Time: 10 minutes.

Description: creamy and delicious

INGREDIENTS:

4 tablespoons unbleached and unenriched flour

1/2 cup almond milk

4 tablespoons soy free earth balance margarine

1 cup vegan cream cheese

1 teaspoon vanilla flavor

5 cups organic powdered sugar

2 tablespoons almond milk only if needed

DIRECTIONS:

Put the flour and almond milk in a small pot and whisk briskly to remove lumps. Once the lumps are dissolved, put the mixture on top of the stove on medium/high burner and whisk briskly continuously until a paste forms and it takes about 25 seconds.

Remove the pot from the heat and stir. Let flour mixture cool off. Remove mixture to a bowl. Then add the earth balance and semi-soft cream cheese and stir with a spoon to mix everything together. Then beat well on low speed with electric mixer and add the flavor and confection sugar a little at a time and beat until fluffy. Continue until all confection sugar is used.

Add milk a drop at a time, if needed and stir with the mixer or a spoon until you have desired to spread on cake.

Optional: For a color swirl mix, 1/8 teaspoon beet powder in a half cup of the frosting and mix well. Use the swirl after frosting the cake.

Cool the cake completely before frosting then the frosting won't run off the cake.

Preparation items: large bowl, electric mixer, measuring cups, large plate and spoons spatula, cup and large spoon

Creamy southern flair macaroni and cheese

Serves: 10. Preparation Time: 15 minutes. Cooking Time: 20 minutes. Total Time: 35 minutes.

Description: This is a great dish. It is creamy and taste great with the buttered bread crumbs on top

INGREDIENTS:

1 block of daiya vegan cheese

16 ounce box organic brown rice macaroni

Dash of cayenne pepper

1 teaspoon garlic powder

4 cups almond milk

1/4 teaspoon sea salt

1/3 piece of red bell pepper

1 slice of gluten free dark rye bread

1 tablespoon soft original earth balance spread

1/2 teaspoon paprika for top

DIRECTIONS:

Preheat oven to 400.

Ground the bell pepper very fine in food processor and set aside.

Grind the cheese and set aside.

Grind the bread and soft margarine very fine in the food processor set aside.

Follow directions on the box for cooking the macaroni.

When the macaroni is cooked, drain macaroni in colander.

Put the hot macaroni in large bowl and add 1/2 of the grounded cheese to the hot macaroni.

Add the cheese sauce, bell pepper and seasonings to the macaroni and mix well. No cheese sauce

Taste and add more seasoning if needed. Pour into large deep baking dish.

Sprinkle the saved cheese, bread crumbs over the top of the macaroni then sprinkle the paprika on top.

Bake for 20 minutes or until began to bubble and then take out of oven serve hot.

Preparation items: large pot, measuring spoons, measuring cup, large deep oblong baking dish, large bowl, knife, food processor.

Curried chic less protein chunks

Serves: 8.   Preparation time: 25 minutes.   Cooking time: 45 minutes.
Total time: 1 hour +10 minutes.

Description: This is a delicious dish and excellent meat substitute.

INGREDIENTS:

3 cups presoaked chicken not textured vegetable protein chunks

1/2 red bell pepper cored, washed and cubed thin

1/3 cup grape seed oil

1 Stalk of fresh celery

1/2 yellow onions

3 cloves garlic

1 teaspoon grounded ginger

1 medium jalapeño pepper deseeded

3-1/3 tablespoons Jamaican curry powder

1 tablespoon grounded cumin

2 tablespoons grounded turmeric

3 tablespoons Bragg's liquid amino or sea salt to taste

1/2 Gallon spring water

DIRECTIONS:

Soak protein chunks overnight in a bowl or for 30 minutes in very hot water.

Squeeze out the water and measure out 3 cups.

Freeze leftover protein for later use.

Peel and clean and chop fine all veggies in food processor and set aside.

Put the protein in a large bowl and add the prepared veggies, oil and all of the seasonings and mix well. Put in refrigerator overnight if time permits or let protein mixture sit for 20 minutes to marinate. Transfer protein to a large pot and sauté protein, vegetables and seasonings on medium/low heat for 20 minutes and stir often.

Add 3 cups of water, and bring to a boil then turn heat to medium and cook covered for 25 minutes or until meat is tender. Add more water if needed and continue cooking. Cook protein until the sauce is like gravy.

Turn off heat.

Serve over nutty flavored quinoa or long grain basmati brown rice.

Preparation items: large heavy duty pot with cover, stirring spoon, food processor, large bowl, measuring spoons and cup, knife and cutting board.

Curried chick less chunky vegetable stew

Serves: 8.   Preparation Time: 10 minutes.   Cooking Time: 50 minutes.   Total Time: 60 minutes

Description: Very pleasing and delightful one dish meal

INGREDIENTS:

3 cups presoaked textured vegetable protein chunks

1 medium onion peeled and chopped

3 fresh carrots washed, peeled and sliced

3 washed, peeled and cubed red potatoes

1 red bell pepper washed, cored and cubed

1 stalk celery washed and chopped

1/3 cup olive oil

3 garlic cloves crushed in food processor

1/3 teaspoon hot red pepper seeds

2 tablespoons Jamaican curry powder

2 tablespoons turmeric

3 tablespoons Bragg's liquid amino or sea salt to taste

1 cup coconut milk

1/2 Gallon spring water

DIRECTIONS:

Soak protein chunks overnight or for 30 minutes in very hot water.

Squeeze out the water and measure out 3 cups. Freeze leftover protein for later use.

Put the protein in a large pot, add prepared garlic, onions, celery, bell pepper, and all of the seasonings, oil and mix well and sauté for 5 minutes on low heat.

Stir often to keep protein from sticking.

Add 2-1/2 cups of water and bring to a boil then lower heat and cook covered on medium heat for 20 minutes

Add the sliced carrots, milk and cubed potatoes and cook for 25 minutes and the stew are lightly thick. Serve hot.

Preparation items: medium heavy duty pot, stirring spoon, large bowl, measuring spoons and cup, knife, food processor and cutting board.

Curried no beef bites stew

Serves: 8.   Preparation Time: 8 minutes.   Cooking Time: 60
minutes.   Total Time: 68 minutes

Description: When cooked, the protein is very tender and delicious and
complements any dish. Always soak enough for freezing.

INGREDIENTS:

3 cups presoaked no beef bites protein tips

1 medium onion peeled and rinsed

4 garlic cloves peeled rinsed

1 stalk of fresh celery rinsed

1 small red bell pepper washed

1 tablespoon grape seed oil

1/4 teaspoon cayenne pepper powder or more if desired

2 tablespoons turmeric powder

2 tablespoons Jamaican curry powder

1 sprig fresh grounded thyme leaves

3 tablespoons Bragg's liquid amino

1 gallon spring water

DIRECTIONS:

Soak protein overnight or 30 minutes in a bowl of boiling hot water. Squeeze out the water and measure out 3 cups.

Freeze leftover protein for later use.

Wash all vegetables before using. After washing the thyme, destem.

Put onion, thyme leaves and garlic, in food processor and chop fine

Cube or slice the celery and bell pepper with the a sharp knife

Put the protein in a large pot and add the prepared veggies, oil and all of the seasonings and Sauté protein on medium/low heat for 15 minutes or until protein start to get brown. Stir often.

Add 3 cups of water and cook covered on medium heat for 45 minutes.

Taste and add more seasonings if desired.

Serve over cooked long grain basmati brown rice recipe or any cooked grain or noodles.

Preparation items: large stainless steel pot, stirring spoon, food processor, large bowl, measuring spoons and cup, knife and cutting board.

*If desired: to thicken, mix 1 tablespoon arrowroot with 3 tablespoons water and cook for 5 minutes more.

Delicate steamed broccoli & almonds

Serves: 4.   Preparation Time: 7 minutes.   Cooking Time: 5 minutes.   Total time: 12 minutes

Description: Beautiful steam broccoli and almonds and gluten free.

INGREDIENTS:

1 fresh head of broccoli cut broccoli into medium spears.

1/3 crushed gluten free dry roasted almonds

1/8 teaspoon cayenne pepper optional

1/8 teaspoon garlic powder

1/8 teaspoon onion powder

2 teaspoons cold pressed olive oil

1/3cup spring water

DIRECTIONS:

Soak broccoli for 5 minutes in cold spring water then drain broccoli and rinse.

Put the prepared broccoli into a medium size pot.

Add the water, pepper, onion powder and garlic powder and stir to mix the broccoli and seasonings.

Turn heat to high and let broccoli come to a boil, then turn off heat and cover and steam on the hot burner for 8 minutes. Only then, remove from the hot burner and add oil, almonds and leave covered.

Watch broccoli closely.

Broccoli is very delicate so don't overcook!

Serve warm.

This dish is delicious with any main course.

Preparation items: medium size pot with lid, food processor, colander, cutting board, measuring spoons and cups, knife.

Delicious vegan raisins and nuts carrot muffins

Serve: 10. Preparation time: 15 minutes. Cooking time: 36 minutes total time: 45 minutes

Description: these muffins are nutritious and healthy with lots of nuts and raisins and less sugar

INGREDIENTS:

2-1/2cups light spelt flour

1 teaspoon grounded all spice

2 tablespoons grounded blond flaxseeds

4 tablespoons spring water

2 teaspoons aluminum-free baking powder

1/2 teaspoon aluminum-free baking soda

1/4teaspoon sea salt

1cup pure maple syrup

1 cup crushed walnuts

1 cup raisins

1-1/2cups grounded carrots

2 teaspoons alcohol free vanilla flavoring

1/2cup original almond milk

1/2 cup soft vegan margarine

1 can non-stick organic olive oil spray

DIRECTIONS:

Preheat oven to 350 degree.

Put paper muffin cups in the holes of the pan and spray with non-stick spray and set aside.

Mix flaxseeds and water together and set aside.

Chop walnuts and set aside.

Wash and peel carrots and put them in the food processor and ground very fine and set aside in a container.

Mix all dry ingredients in a medium bowl.

Mix well the carrots, flaxseed mixture, olive oil, margarine, almond milk and flavor in the blender.

Slowly add the wet ingredients to the dry ingredients and mix with a large spoon just to get everything moist.

Add walnuts pieces, raisins and mix just until all is mixed in.

Use large spoon to fill muffin cups 2/3 full and bake for 36 minutes, then insert long tooth pick in center to see if comes out clean. If uncooked batter is on tooth pick cook 3-4 minutes and test again. A few dry crumbs are okay.

Preparation items: large bowl, large measuring cup, measuring cup and spoons, nonstick large muffin pans, white muffin paper cups, large mixing spoon and food processor, blender

Delicious homemade meatless spaghetti sauce

Serves: 8.   Preparation Time: 10 minutes.   Cooking Time: 53minutes. Total Time: 63 minutes

Description: This spaghetti sauce taste great with lots of veggies. This Sauce can be frozen for use later

I always soak a lot of soy protein granules and freeze them in 2 cup portions. If using plantains or tofu, do not freeze spaghetti sauce.

INGREDIENTS:

2cups presoaked granules textured vegetable protein with water squeezed out; if frozen thaw out before using. If in a hurry, presoak the vegetable protein in 4 cups of boiling hot water for 30 minutes and squeeze the water out before using recipe. Leftover protein can be frozen.

1 tablespoon grounded oregano flakes

2 tablespoons grounded basil flakes

4 large cloves fresh garlic peeled and rinsed

1- large fresh onion peeled and rinsed

2 sprigs of fresh cilantro or 1 teaspoon dried cilantro

2 large fresh tomatoes washed grounded in food processor

1 fresh red bell pepper cored washed and chopped

1-large fresh carrot washed and chopped

2 tablespoons grounded paprika

1/4cup regular olive oil

1-24 ounce jar rega organic gluten free Italian tomato puree

2-6 ounce cans Woodstock gluten free organic tomato paste

2 tablespoons organic agave nectar

1/4 teaspoon cayenne pepper

2 cups spring water

2 tablespoons Bragg's liquid amino

DIRECTIONS:

Grind the onion, garlic and carrot very fine in food processor and set aside.

Soak tomatoes in boiling hot water for 3 minutes, then poke and peel off skin and grind tomatoes and fresh cilantro in food processor very fine and set aside.

Chop the red bell pepper with a knife and set aside.

Then sauté prepared veggies and presoaked protein and all of the seasonings in large pot with olive oil for 3 minutes on medium heat, stirring often.

Mix the tomato paste, tomatoes, tomato puree and water together in a bowl then add to the pot and stir thoroughly.

Cook covered pot and cook on top of the stove for 35 minutes on medium heat.

Stir in sweetener and simmer for 20 minutes on low heat.

Stir often, taste and add more seasoning if needed.

Serve over spaghetti or Capellini.

Soy parmesan cheese can be sprinkled over spaghetti dish.

Preparation items: 1-large heavy duty stainless steel pot, food processor, measuring spoons and cup, large stirring spoons, can opener, medium bowl and knife.

For variety: small cubed extra firm organic tofu sautéed on top of the stove in a non-stick pan with a teaspoon Bragg's liquid amino and 1-tablespoon olive oil. Sauté until tofu are well browned then add to spaghetti sauce.

Another variety: add medium sliced cauliflower to the sauce in the last 8 minutes.

Delicious masala tomato flavored tofu

Serves: 4. Preparation Time: 20 minutes. Cooking Time: 24 minutes. Total Time: 45 minutes.

Description: Colorful and delicious

This is a quick and easy dish to make when in a hurry.

INGREDIENTS:

1 block extra firm organic sprouted tofu, rinsed and cut in 4 slices and cut the slices in half making 8 pieces

1/4 cup extra virgin olive oil

1/2 onion peeled rinsed sliced

2 small mushroom portabella peeled and rinsed and sliced

1 red bell pepper cored rinsed and chopped

2 fresh organic tomatoes rinsed and chopped

1 carrot rinsed and sliced

1 teaspoon paprika

1/8 teaspoon cayenne pepper

1 teaspoon turmeric

3 tablespoons Bragg's liquid amino

1/2 cup organic gluten and fructose free ketchup

2 tablespoons masala chicken seasoning

6 tablespoons olive oil

DIRECTIONS:

Soak tomatoes in boiling hot water for 3 minutes then remove the skin and chop small.

Prepare the other vegetables and set aside

In a small bowl, mix Braggs liquid amino, masala chicken seasoning, turmeric, paprika and cayenne pepper. Place prepared tofu in a large bowl and pour the mixture over the tofu and let marinate for 15 minutes. Save the marinating mixture and mix in with the ketchup and set aside.

Place a non- stick fry pan on top of the stove on medium heat then put in 3 tbsp olive oil and put in the prepared veggies and sauté them for 3 minutes careful not to let them burn. Remove veggies to a plate.

Place the marinated tofu pieces in the same pan and add 3 tbsp oil and let the side get brown takes about 4 minutes for each side to get brown.

Continue until all of tofu is cooked and browned well.

When the tofu is cooked place the vegetables on top of the tofu and pour the marinating mixture with the ketchup on top of the veggies and tofu. Sprinkle on some paprika and simmer for 5 minutes uncovered. Serve hot.

Preparation items: large non-stick frying pan, measuring spoons and cup, plate, flipper, small bowl, large bowl, knife and cutting board.

Delightful tossed salad

Serves: 8. Preparation Time: 15 minutes. Mixing Time: 5 minutes. Total Time: 20 minutes.

Description: This is a great salad that has different color veggies that's healthy and it compliments any dinner

INGREDIENTS:

1 Organic unpeeled cucumber

8 green tip lettuce leaves

1/2 cup grape tomatoes

1/2 piece of radicchio

2 cup spring mix

1 small purple onion

DIRECTIONS:

Wash the green leaf lettuce, radicchio and slice thin. Peel and rinse the onion. Rinse and slice the grape tomatoes in half or if using roma tomatoes rinse and cube them. Rinse the spring mix. Put the prepared salad in a salad spinner to remove the water.

Remove the salad makings from the spinner to a large bowl and toss lightly.

Wash the cucumber and cut in half and slice thin and set aside on paper towel.

Place the slice cucumbers on sides and top of the salad.

Serve with the creamy carrot supreme salad dressing.

For variety, add a cubed baby yellow squash.

Preparation items: salad spinner, large salad bowl, serving tongs, cutting board, sharp knife, paper towels, measuring cup and spoons.

Egg-less picnic potato salad

Serves: 10.   Preparation Time: 20 minutes.   Cooking Time: 30
minutes.   Total Time: 50 minutes

Description: Delightful potato salad that is creamy and delicious

My family talks about my potato salad to their friends. This potato
salad is low in fat and cholesterol and I leave the skins on when boiling
because it gives the potato salad more flavors.

INGREDIENTS:

6-organic large red potatoes washed

1 gallon spring water

1 tablespoon light agave nectar

1/2 red bell pepper

1/3 piece green bell pepper

1/3 piece yellow bell pepper

1/2 stalk celery

1 small purple onion

2 pinches of cayenne pepper

1 teaspoon sea salt or to taste

3/4cup organic sweet relish, drained

1 teaspoon grounded turmeric

1 tablespoon light agave nectar

3cups just mayo by Hamilton creek

1/2 teaspoon grounded paprika reserve for sprinkling on top of potato salad

DIRECTIONS:

Put washed unpeeled potatoes in a large pot with enough water to cover them.

Boil the potatoes on top of the stove on high heat until they began to boil, then reduce heat to medium and boil for 30 minutes or until a for can go through potatoes.

Wash all vegetables and dry them.

Peel the onion and use half.

Use food processor to chop vegetables, onion and set aside in a container lined with paper towels.

Drain the sweet relish in a strainer.

When you are able to handle the potatoes, peel off skins and cut into cubes and put them in a large bowl. Add in the prepared veggies, pepper, sea salt, relish, turmeric, agave nectar, just mayo and mix well.

Taste and add more seasonings and just mayo if needed. Put potato salad in a clean bowl and sprinkle paprika over the top and decorate with sprigs of fresh washed dry parsley. Refrigerate before serving.

Preparation items: large stainless steel pot, 2-large bowls, container, large spoon, wooden stirring spoon, measuring spoons and cups cutting board and knife.

Flavorful vegan lasagna

Serves 12.   Preparation Time: 25 minutes.   Cooking Time: 45 Total Time: 1hr + 10 minutes

Description: This is a great one dish casserole that is nutritional and delicious so enjoy!

INGREDIENTS:

1/4 cup olive oil

4 sprigs fresh parsley stems cut off and rinsed well

4 fresh garlic cloves peeled and rinsed

1 large purple onion peeled and rinsed

1/4 teaspoon cayenne pepper

1 tablespoon whole dried basil

1 tablespoon dried oregano

1 tablespoon dried cilantro or 2 sprigs fresh cilantro

2 tablespoons paprika powder

1/4cup Bragg's liquid amino

2cups Gardein gluten-free beefless ground

2- 24oz jars rega gluten free organic tomato puree

1can organic Muir cherry tomatoes

1 tablespoon organic light agave nectar

12 ounce package vegan whole wheat lasagna noodles

2 bunch fresh spinach

1 cup sliced mushrooms

1 Block organic sprouted extra firm tofu

1- Block vegan daiya mozzarella cheese

1 block vegan diaya cheddar cheese

1 can vegan grated parmesan cheese

DIRECTIONS:

Pre heat oven 375 degrees

Chop garlic, parsley and onion and destem cilantro. If using fresh, put in food processor until very fine and set aside.

Rinse the mushrooms and dry them.

Soak the spinach in water for 5 minutes, then drain and rinse well and use a salad spinner to get out the water and set aside.

In a large non-stick frying pan, add olive oil, finely chopped garlic, parsley, onion, dry seasonings, liquid amino, beefless ground and sauté on top of stove for 3 minutes.

Add the tomato puree, cherry tomatoes and let the sauce come to a boil on top of stove, then turn the heat to low and let simmer for 15 minutes. Then add the sweetener and stir.

Meanwhile cook the lasagna noodles according to the package directions in the large pot, then drain and rinse with cool water.

Put the prepared spinach and sliced mushrooms in a medium pot on top of the stove steam for 5 minutes drain off liquid.

Chop the tofu, mozzarella and cheddar cheese in the food processor and save 1-cup for the top of the lasagna.

Now add 2 cups of sauce to the bottom of baking pan. Arrange the noodles to cover the sauce then spread some of the cheese tofu mixture and sautéed vegetables evenly over the noodles and with a dipper spread generously more sauce.

Repeat layers and end with noodles and balance of sauce on top.

Sprinkle the reserved cup of cheese tofu mixture over the top of lasagna and sprinkle on some parmesan cheese. Bake in the oven for 45 minutes or until the top is light brown. Serve warm.

Preparation items: large stainless steel baking pan, large nonstick fry pan, 2 medium pot, food processor, cutting board, knife, measuring cups and spoons, dipper, colander

Variety: without the beefless ground use small cubed baby Indian eggplants.

Raw creamy cucumber salad dressing

Yield 16 oz Preparation Time: 3 minutes blending Time: 3 minutes
Total Time: 6 minutes

Description: creamy and delicious as a dip or spread over salad

INGREDIENTS:

1/2 fresh organic cucumber, unpeeled

3tablespoons pure maple syrup

1/4 teaspoon sea salt

Pinch of cayenne pepper

2 tablespoons grounded flaxseed

1teaspoon poppy seeds

1/4cup Bragg's apple cider vinegar or juice from 1-1/2 lemons

1/2cup extra virgin olive oil

Small piece of onion

1 garlic clove

1 cup almond milk added last to rinse out blender

DIRECTIONS:

Rinse veggies and put all of above ingredients in duty blender and blend until creamy about 3 minutes

Taste and add more seasoning if needed. Pour dressing into medium container and rinse out the blender with the milk and pour into the dressing and store in the refrigerator.

If the dressing is two thick add a little more almond milk or water.

Preparation items needed: heavy duty blender, strainer, measuring cup and spoons, knife, cutting board and medium container with lid.

Garlic no turkey breast

Serves 10 Preparation Time: 20 minutes Cooking Time 45minutes total time 1hour+ 5 minutes

Description: Excellent no turkey replacement that taste good

INGREDIENTS:

6 Packs organic firm tofu

2 tablespoons onion powder

3-tablespoons garlic powder

1 tablespoon Bragg's liquid amino

1//3 teaspoon red pepper seeds

1/3 cup extra virgin olive oil

6-tablespoons broth powder-no chicken

For basting:

Mix ingredients below together in a measuring cup and set aside

1/2 teaspoon garlic powder

1/2 teaspoon onion powder

1/4cup vegetable broth-page 266

1drop gravy master liquid

1 tablespoon melted earth balance buttery spread

1/3 cup Bragg's liquid amino

DIRECTIONS:

Preheat oven to 375 degrees

In a large bowl, mash the tofu, a pack at a time with a potato masher or hands making sure the tofu is mashed very well. Add the broth powder -no chicken mix, onion powder, garlic powder, olive oil and continue to mash and mix in the seasoning together thoroughly with the completely mashed tofu.

Cut an extra- large piece of cheese cloth and put the opened up cheese cloth in the large flat pan.

Dump prepared tofu mixture into the cheese cloth and gather the cheese cloth with the tofu inside.

Twist the top of the cloth together very tight and tie.

Set the bundle of tofu in the colander and set the colander on top of a medium plastic container so the tofu mixture can drain off the liquid.

Set a heavy object on top of tofu and let drain overnight. I use a brick wrapped in aluminum foil.

Next day carefully take the cheese cloth off the tofu and put into oblong baking pan.

With hands shape the loaf to look like a turkey breast indenting the middle of the tofu with the side of your hand.

Pour half of basting mix over the breast and bake for 20 minutes uncovered, take breast out of oven and pour the remaining basting mix over the breast and continue cooking for 25 minutes or until nicely browned.

Serve with brown gravy

Preparation items: large wide bowl, potato masher, measuring spoons and cups, cheese cloth, colander, medium plastic container, large flat pan, clean heavy object, string to tie and scissors.

Golden brown gravy

Yield: 3 cups Preparation Time: 4 minutes Cooking Time: 15 minutes
Total Time: 19 minute

Description: This gravy is tasty and can complement any dish that calls
for gravy.

INGREDIENTS:

1/8 cup earth balance spread and 2 tablespoon olive oil

4 tablespoons spelt flour

1 tablespoon broth powder-no chicken mix

3tablespoons nutritional yeast flakes

1 teaspoon paprika powder

1 teaspoon onion powder

1/2 teaspoon garlic powder

2 pinches cayenne pepper

4cups vegetable broth-page 266

2 tablespoons liquid amino

DIRECTIONS:

Put the nutritional yeast, flour, vegetable powdered broth mix, paprika, onion powder, garlic powder and cayenne pepper in a small bowl and mix together and set aside.

Put olive oil and earth balance spread in fry pan on top of the stove and let it get warm then add the flour mixture and stir constantly until the mixture start to get brown takes 2 minutes on medium heat then slowly add 1 cup of the vegetable broth whisking constantly to prevent lumps. Once everything is mix in and the gravy is gently boiling stir and add the 3 cups remaining broth.

Add the liquid amino and stir.

If for some reason the gravy is lumpy just put it in the blender and blend until the gravy is smooth then put the gravy back into the pan and continue to cook.

The gravy will be thin at first but cook for 10 minutes to start thicken.

Turn the heat to medium low.

Continue to cook and stir until gravy is at desired thickness. If gravy is too thick add a little water to get desired thickness.

Taste and add more seasoning if needed.

Preparation items needed: large heavy duty stainless steel fry pan, medium bowl, fork, measuring cup and spoons, Blender, large stirring spoon or whisker.

Gourmet vegan salad

Serves: 10 Preparation Time: 10 minutes mixing Time: 10 minute Total Time: 20 minute

Description: super colorful salad fit for any occasion

INGREDIENTS:

1/2 head of romaine lettuce

1/2 head of red tip lettuce

1pack grape tomatoes

1 purple onion

1 cucumber

1 small zucchini

1 package alfalfa sprouts

1/2 cup pitted black olives chop slightly and add last

1/2 cup golden raisins add last

1/2cup carrot shreds

DIRECTIONS:

Wash all veggies very well and drain

Soak the alfalfa sprouts for 5 minutes the rise and drain.

Slice the lettuce in small pieces.

Thinly slice the onion and save some for the top.

Slice the tomatoes in half and save some for the top.

Cut the zucchini and cucumber in half then slice in thin slices and save a few slices for the top.

Cube the red pepper

When all of the salad makings are prepared put half of the salad in the spinner and spin out the water then put salad into a large salad bowl.

Continue spinning the other half of the salad until all of the salad is spent and the water is whisked out. Put the salad into the salad bowl.

Toss the salad to mix then sprinkle and arrange the saved item on top and sprinkle some alfalfa sprouts on top. Now you have a beautiful salad for any occasion.

Preparation items: salad spinner, large bowl, measuring cups and spoons cutting board, sharp knife.

Great breakfast oatmeal with blue berries n bananas

Serves: 4 Preparation Time: 5 minutes Cooking Time: 15 minutes Total Time 20 minutes

Description: Creamy and hearty and delicious

Eating oatmeal is a good way to start your day.

It is low in fat and a good source of protein and fiber. Add blueberries and bananas for a complete breakfast

INGREDIENTS:

2 cups organic rolled oats

3cups purified water

Grounded flaxseeds

Almond milk

Silk vanilla cream

Ripe bananas

Blueberries

DIRECTIONS:

Put the water in a pot and put on the stove and let the water come to a boil then add the oats and stir. Turn the heat to low and cover the pot and let the oats cook for15 minutes. Turn off the heat and let the cooked oats sit for 2 minutes. Serve warm with blueberries, sliced bananas, flax seeds, cream and almond milk.

Preparation items: medium heavy duty pot with lid, stirring spoon, knife, measuring cup and spoons

Great buttermilk pancakes

Serves: 6 Preparation Time: 8 minutes Cooking Time: 20 minutes
Total Time: 28 minutes

Description: Mouth-watering pancakes served with scramble tofu

INGREDIENTS:

2cups spelt flour

2tablespoons grounded sunflower seeds

1/2 cup raisins

2 tablespoons grounded flax seeds mixed with 4 tablespoons warm spring water

3teaspoons pure maple syrup

1/4 teaspoon sea salt- optional

3 teaspoons aluminum free baking powder

1/2 teaspoon aluminum free baking soda

2-1/2cups original almond milk mixed with 1 tablespoon Bragg's apple cider vinegar

1/4cup olive oil

1 bottle pure maple syrup or your choice of syrup

1 can nonstick organic olive oil spray

DIRECTIONS:

Heat the pancake griddle to 375

Put all dry ingredients in a large measuring cup and stir well.

Mix flax seeds and water and let sit for 3 minutes

Mix milk, vinegar together and let sit for 3 minutes

Put all wet ingredients and oil in a blender and mix together.

Add the wet ingredients to the dry ingredients and mix together until most of the lumps are gone.

Let batter sit for 1 minute then stir again.

If the batter is thick add a little milk.

Spray pancake griddle with organic nonstick spray.

Put 1/4cup pancake mix on the grill

Cook pancakes until both sides is brown.

Tip: Flip pancakes when the top began to look dry.

Pancakes can be served with pats of earth balance spread put in between each pancake and topped with maple syrup or your choice of syrup

Preparation items needed: non-stick pancake griddle, measuring cups and spoons, large and small bowls, pancake flipper, cutting board, knife, large plate and butter knife.

Variety: peeled and chopped apples and walnut pieces can be added on top of pancakes.

Great steamed plantains

Serves: 8 minutes Preparation Time: 8 minutes Cooking Time: 30 minutes Total Time: 38 minutes

Description: cooked ripe plantains are very delicious and have a sweet taste. They can be mashed with a little vegan margarine and used in place of mashed potatoes.

INGREDIENTS:

4 ripe plantains peeled

16 ounces can organic crushed tomatoes

1 teaspoon whole dried basil

1 teaspoon dried oregano

1/4 teaspoon real sea salt

1 teaspoon grounded paprika

2 teaspoons olive oil

1 cup spring water

DIRECTIONS:

Peel the plantains and cut them into thirds.

Put in a medium pot and rinse the plantains.

Add one cup spring water and the seasonings and tomatoes.

Cover the pot and steam on medium heat for 25 minutes

Taste and add more seasoning if needed, add the oil and keep lid on for 5 minutes

Serve as a side dish.

Preparation items: medium heavy duty pot, measuring spoons and cups, knife and cutting board

Green energy salad

Serves: 8 Preparation Time: 19 minutes mixing Time: 8 minutes Total
Time: 27 minute
Description: this salad is energizing and colorful

INGREDIENTS:

6 Leaves of fresh spinach washed, sliced and drain

5 leaves of romaine lettuce

1 cup of spring mix washed and drained

1-carrots rinsed and coarsely grounded in food processor

1-Small fresh purple onion peeled rinsed and sliced thin

1/2 fresh red bell pepper cored rinsed and cubed

1cup Fresh alfalfa sprouts rinsed and drained

1/4 cup dried raisins

1-fresh organic cucumber rinsed and sliced

1-fresh tomato rinsed and cubed

6 fresh strawberries

1 avocado rinsed peeled and sliced thin

1 cup raw walnuts

DIRECTIONS:

Thoroughly wash all of the veggies and let them drain or spin in a salad spinner.

Spread in layers half of the sliced spinach leaves, lettuce, alfalfa sprouts and spring mix in the salad bowl.

Spread in the shredded carrots, the sliced purple onions, and cubed red bell pepper.

Now spread in the remaining spinach, spring mix, alfalfa sprouts.

Then layer the sliced cucumbers around the side of the salad and spread the small slices of tomatoes and avocado around the sides of the cucumbers.

Put walnuts and raisins over individual salads when it's ready to be served.

Use garlic and tomato salad dressing on page 34 or your favorite salad dressing as a topping.

For variety sprinkle alfalfa sprouts on top

Preparation items needed: colander large salad bowl, serving tongs, cutting board, sharp knife, measuring cup and spoons, food processor.

Grilled tofu steaks

Serves: 6 Preparation Time: 10 minutes Cooking Time: 20 minutes
Total Time: 30 minutes

Description: Beautiful grilled steaks that make a quick lunch or
barbeque as a main dish

INGREDIENTS:

2 packs extra firm organic tofu

1/3 cup Bragg's liquid amino

2teaspoons ground turmeric

1 tablespoon dry mustard powder

1 teaspoon onion powder

1 teaspoon garlic powder

1-1/2teaspoon ground paprika

1/2 cup extra virgin olive oil

1/4 teaspoon of cayenne pepper

DIRECTIONS:

Turn pancake grill to 375 degrees

Slice the tofu the long way into medium slices about 6 slices for each block of tofu and set aside.

Put all of dry ingredients in a pepper shaker.

Put the oil and liquid amino in a medium cup and stir well.

Now put the sliced tofu on the grill and shake half of the dry seasonings over the tofu steaks then with a spoon dip some of the oil and liquid amino mixture over the steaks.

Cook the tofu steaks on first side until they are brown about 4 minutes.

Then turn tofu over and shake balance of the dry seasoning over the steaks and dip the balance of the oil and liquid amino mixture over the tofu steaks and continue cooking until brown about 4 minutes.

Turn again and cook for 2 minutes on each side

Remove from the grill and put the tofu into a serving plate on paper towels.

Steaks can be served hot as a sandwich on whole wheat bread topped with vegenaise sandwich spread, lettuce and sliced tomatoes and sliced purple onions, vegan cheese and sprouts.

Preparation items: indoor pancake grill, knife, measuring cups and spoons, cutting board, medium cup, pepper shaker, serving plate and flat knife.

Vegan southern style collard greens with carrots

Serves: 10 Preparation Time: 25 minutes Cooking Time 45 minutes
Total Time: 1 hr+10 minutes

Description: These greens and carrots are so tender and delicious
without meat and they are healthy with lots of minerals and vitamins.
Collard greens are vegetables that are the oldest members of the
cabbage family, but are also close relatives to kale. They are at their
best after the frost.

INGREDIENTS:

3 Bunches organic collard greens picked washed

4 tablespoon olive oil

1 tablespoon Bragg's apple cider vinegar

1/4 teaspoon cayenne pepper powder

1 small onion chopped small

1 teaspoon garlic powder

1/2package baby carrots rinsed and sliced

3 cups spring water

1/2 teaspoon sea salt or to taste

DIRECTIONS:

Picked and cut off the large stems from the greens and save for smoothie.

Then wash the leaves thoroughly about 2 or 3 times in a clean sink and let them drain.

When greens are drained slice them into thin slices.

Afterwards transfer them to a large pot.

Add the water and all of the seasonings (except the salt, carrots and olive oil).

Stir greens to mix the seasoning, greens and onions together.

Cook on top of stove on high until began to boil.

Turn heat to medium and cook for 40 minutes or until tender.

Stir greens occasionally.

Taste, add more seasoning if needed and add the carrots and cook for another 10 minutes.

Turn off heat and stir in the salt, olive oil and serve warm.

Preparation items needed: large heavy-duty stainless steel pot, measuring cups and spoons, stainless steel colander, sharp knife, chopping board and large deep basin or clean sink.

Healthy whole grain millet

Serves: 4 Preparation Time 5minutes Cooking Time: 25 minutes
Total Time: 30 minutes

Description: Millet is an ancient African and Asian grain and can be used instead of rice and is a high source of fiber. It has a sweet nutty flavor Millet is gluten free.

INGREDIENTS:

1 cup millet rinsed and drained

1-1/3cup spring water

2 tablespoon olive oil

1 tablespoon Bragg's liquid amino

6 cloves if desired

DIRECTIONS:

Wash and drain the millet well set aside

Put the seasoning in the water and let water come to a boil in a medium pot on top of the stove. Then put the millet in to the boiling water. Turn heat to medium low and cover the pot and simmer on low heat for 20 minutes on top of the stove do not stir nor open the pot during the cooking process. After 20 minutes check the millet to see if done and if needed add 1/4 cup of water and keep covered and steam for a few minutes then fluff the millet and keep the pot cover and let the millet sit for 2 minutes before serving.

Serve with any recipe that calls for rice.

Variety: for a colorful dish add a few slivers of shredded carrots and a few raisins during the cooking process

Preparation item: medium pot, measuring cup and spoons, small holed strainer and large spoon.

Hearty and bold old fashion vegetarian soup

Serves: 8 Preparation Time: 20 minutes Cooking Time: 40 minutes
  Total Time: 1 hour

Description: awesome vegetable soup that is hearty and delicious

INGREDIENTS:

4 fingerling potatoes peeled and cubed medium

9 cups spring water

2-1/2 tablespoons liquid amino

1 cup green peas

3 cloves of garlic peeled, rinsed

1 small onion peeled and rinsed

6 string beans washed cut small

4 peeled sliced and rinsed mushrooms

3 dinosaur kale leaves washed and slice thin

2 fresh carrot rinsed and sliced

1/2 cup rinsed cubed red bell pepper

2 large tomatoes washed peeled and chopped

1 fresh ears of corn rinsed and cut off the cob

1 small cauliflower washed, sliced

1 tablespoon grounded turmeric

1 fresh sprig of rosemary washed and de stemmed

1 teaspoon grounded paprika

1 sprig fresh oregano washed and de stemmed

1/4teaspoon grounded cayenne pepper

1 tablespoon olive oil

1 tablespoon agave nectar

DIRECTIONS:

Put the 8 cups of water on top of the stove on high heat and add all of the dry ingredients and liquid amino and let the pot come to a light boil then turn heat to medium.

Put the onions, garlic, oregano leaves, rosemary leaves in a food processor and grind very fine and add to the pot.

Put tomatoes in boiling hot water for 3 minutes then peel off skin and chop fine in food processor and add to the soup.

Put the prepared carrots, mushrooms, potatoes, string beans, dinosaur kale leaves to the pot and cook for 20 minutes on medium heat and stir often.

Then add to the pot prepared corn, bell pepper, agave nectar and cauliflower.

Continue to cook on medium heat for 20 minutes

Taste and add oil and more seasons if desired and stir well.

1 tablespoon potato starch can be stirred into 1/4 cup spring water to thicken if desired add last and cook for 5 minutes. Serve hot.

Preparation items: large stainless steel pot with lid, sharp knife, measuring cup and spoons, large stirring spoon, cutting board and food Processor.

Hearty vegetables, tofu and red potato soup

Serves: 10 Preparation Time: 15 minutes Cooking Time: minutes 35 minutes Total Time: 50 minutes

Description: This soup is a Hearty winter soup but can be enjoyed anytime. It have lots of veggies that is healthy and enjoyable

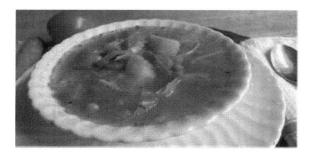

INGREDIENTS:

2 Roma tomatoes rinsed

1/2 onion peeled and rinsed

2 peeled, rinsed garlic cloves

1 rutabaga peeled washed and cubed in small cubes

2-1/2 tablespoon liquid amino

1 pack firm sprouted tofu rinsed and cubed

2red potatoes washed and cubed

1/3 piece of cabbage rinsed well and sliced in medium pieces

1/2 red bell pepper rinsed, cubed

2 carrots rinsed and sliced

1/2 teaspoon maple syrup add in last

1 small pack green sweet peas add last

1/8 teaspoon cayenne pepper optional

1 tablespoon turmeric add last

1 tablespoon paprika

1/4 teaspoon dried basil

2 tablespoons olive oil

8 cups spring water

DIRECTIONS:

Cube the peeled rutabaga.

Chop tomatoes, garlic and onion in the food processor very fine.

Put chopped tomatoes, onions, garlic and prepared rutabaga in a large soup pot along with the seasonings.

Add olive oil and sauté for 5 minutes on top of the stove and stir often.

Then add the water, liquid amino, prepared tofu, potatoes, sliced cabbage, bell pepper, carrots and let pot come to a quick boil then cook on medium heat for 25 minutes.

Add green peas, maple syrup and stir well, simmer for 5 minute. Taste and add more seasoning if needed.

Serve hot.

Preparation items: large stainless steel soup pot sharp paring knife, food processor, cutting board, measuring cup and spoons.

Homemade meatless vegetable chili

Serves 15 Preparation Time: 25 minutes Cooking Time: 1 hr +30 minutes Total Time: 1 hr +55 minutes

Description: Spicy, hearty and very satisfying as a one dish meal

Beans are needed to maintain good health. Kidney beans also have specific benefits for your heart and digestive health

INGREDIENTS:

3 cups of presoaked light kidney beans

1-1/2 cups presoaked vegetable protein granules

2 table extra virgin olive oil

1 large onions peeled and rinsed chopped

4 cloves of garlic peeled rinsed and grounded

1 large carrot washed and grounded

1 teaspoon grounded ginger

2 tablespoons cumin, grounded

1/4 teaspoon cayenne pepper more or less if desired

1/8 teaspoon ground chili chipotle – very hot, use sparring

3 tablespoons Bragg's liquid amino

1 tablespoon whole dried basil

1 tablespoon whole dried oregano

2 tablespoons paprika powder

5 tablespoon chili powder

3 fresh large tomatoes rinsed

1 tablespoon sweetener of choice add last

24 ounce jar of rega gluten free organic tomato puree, but only use 16 ounces add last. Save leftover tomato puree.

1 small can Muir organic tomato paste add last

1/2 cup red bell pepper cored rinsed

1/2 cup green bell peppers cored rinsed

1 teaspoon aluminum free baking soda for soaking beans

1 gallon spring water

DIRECTIONS:

Pick out any small stones and rinse real well

Soak beans overnight in water and the baking soda or quick soak if in a hurry. Follow quick soak instruction on the bag but omit baking soda. Rinse beans well before using and measure out 4 cups and freeze leftover deans.

Soak protein overnight in a bowl of spring water or quick soak for 30 minutes in boiling hot water, Squeeze out the water before using and measure out 1-1/2 cups and freeze leftover protein.

Soak tomatoes in a bowl of boiling hot water for 3 minutes then poke and peel of the skin and grind tomatoes fine in food processor before adding to the chili.

Put carrot, onion and garlic in food processor and grind very fine.

Chop the bell peppers and save some for garnishing.

Put the olive oil, beans, protein, seasonings, grounded onions, garlic and carrot to the pot. Add prepared bell pepper and stir.

Put the pot on top of the stove on medium heat and sauté in a table of oil for 10 minutes and stir often to mix everything together.

Add 6 cup water, tomatoes to the pot and gently mix thoroughly.

Start the cooking process on high heat uncovered until the chili bean began to boil then stir and cover and cook on medium heat for 50 minutes or until beans are tender

Stir the chili often to keep it from sticking.

Add last 2 cups of water and tomato puree, tomato paste, sweetener and simmer on low heat for 30 minutes and stir often. Taste and add more liquid amino and cayenne pepper if needed.

Sauté saved bell peppers on top in a tablespoon of olive oil and garnish them on top before serving.

Preparation items: large heavy duty nonstick stainless steel pot with lid, measuring cups and spoons, stirring spoon, sharp knife, cutting board, fry pan and food processor

Kale and poblano green peppers

Serves: 5 Preparation Time: 10 minutes Cooking Time: 30 minutes
Total Time: 40 minutes

Description this is a beautiful and colorful dish that taste good and can
be served with any meal.

INGREDIENTS:

2 bunch fresh kale

1/2 poblano green pepper rinsed and chopped

1/2 medium onion peeled rinsed and chopped

1/2 teaspoon garlic powder

1/2 teaspoon sea salt

1/8 teaspoon grounded cayenne pepper

2 tablespoon olive oil added last

DIRECTIONS:

Picked and washed kale thoroughly

Slice kale medium thin and put in salad spinner to drain off water.

Put the prepared kale, onion, poblano green pepper and all seasonings in medium pot and steam covered for 30 minutes.

Stir in 2 tbsp olive oil.

Serve warm as a side dish.

Preparation items: medium stainless steel pot, stirring spoon, measuring cup and spoons and chopping board.

Lentils and mock chicken protein chunks

Serves: 8 Preparation Time: 10 minutes Cooking Time: 45 minutes Total Time: 55 minutes

Description: This is a quick dish and the taste is excellent. Lentil beans are light and healthy.

INGREDIENTS:

4 cups brown lentil beans pick through and rinsed well

1/2 cup textured vegetable protein chunks

1/2 onion peeled rinsed and chopped

3 cloves of garlic peeled rinsed and chopped

2 Roma tomatoes rinsed and chopped

1/3 teaspoon grounded cayenne pepper optional

1/2 teaspoon grounded cumin

1 teaspoon grounded paprika

2 tablespoon earth balance spread

1 tablespoon extra-virgin olive oil

1-1/2 tablespoons Bragg's liquid amino

1/2 teaspoon grounded poultry seasoning

1 teaspoon grounded turmeric

4 cups spring water, more if needed

DIRECTIONS:

Soak protein overnight in a bowl of spring water or Quick soak in boiling hot water for 30 minutes. Squeeze out water before using and measure out a half of cup. Freeze leftover protein.

Chop vegetables in food processor

Put prepared protein chunks, lentils, seasonings olive oil, earth balance and all of the chopped vegetables in a large pot and sauté on medium heat on top of the stove for 5 minutes stir often so nothing burn or stick to the pot.

Now add the water and turn the heat to high to start boil then to medium and cook for 40 minutes. Stir occasionally. For doneness, mash a bean between the fingers.

If beans are done turn off the heat and serve warm over long grain basaltic rice page or nutty flavored quinoa page 270 or as a soup.

Preparation items: large heavy duty non-stick stainless steel pot with lid, measuring cups and spoons, stirring spoon, sharp knife and cutting board, food processor.

Light and delicious vegan lentil burgers

Serves: 10 Preparation Time: 25 minutes Cooking Time: 40 minutes Total Time: 1hr + 5 minutes

Description: Delicious and healthy

We love these burgers and I cook them often. They are delicious. I spread vegenaise sandwich spread on a burger bun topped with burger, ketchup lettuce, sprouts, tomato, purple onion, spicy brown mustard and sometimes I spread grated vegan cheese over all of the garnishes. Burgers in the picture are fried.

INGREDIENTS:

2cups cooked organic lentil beans

1 fresh carrot rinsed cut in small pieces

1/2 medium onion peeled

1/2 red bell pepper rinsed

4 garlic cloves peeled rinsed

2 teaspoons grounded flax seeds

2 slices toasted spelt bread

1/2cup spelt flour

1 cup raw pumpkin grounded seeds

1/2cup mushrooms rinsed well

1/4 teaspoon grounded cayenne pepper

1/2 teaspoon turmeric powder

1 teaspoon paprika powder

1/2teaspoon grounded paprika

1/2teaspoon grounded sage

2 tablespoons Bragg's liquid amino

1/2 cup cold pressed olive oil

1 can nonstick organic olive oil spray

1/2gallon spring water

DIRECTIONS: Wash and clean 2 cups of lentil beans when cleaned cook lentils in 3 cups of water and 1/2 teaspoon ginger in medium pot on top of stove, cook about 25 minutes. Add more water if needed. Drain off liquid before making burgers and save. Measure out 2 cups and freeze leftover lentils.

Finely grind the pumpkin seeds in food processor and add to the bowl.

Finely grind toasted bread in food processor and add to the bowl.

Add 1/2 cup of lentil beans to the bowl and grind 1-1/2 cups in food processor and add to the bowl.

Grind carrot, bell pepper, garlic in the food processor.

Chop onions with a sharp knife into small pieces.

Chop mushrooms into small pieces.

Sauté chopped mushrooms, onions and grounded vegetables in nonstick pan with 3 tablespoons of oil for one minutes.

And add sautéed vegetables, flaxseeds, seasonings to the bowl and mix.

Add spelt flour liquid amino and mix well until incorporated.

Heat 3 tablespoons of oil in a non-stick fry pan on top of the stove.

Use a large ice cream scooper sprayed with nonstick olive oil spray to scoop the burger mix and place into the pan and place 4 burgers in the heated oil. Cook on medium heat.

When the first side is browned it takes about 4 minutes. Flip the burgers over with pancake turner and lightly flatten. When browned flip over again and continue to cook until browned.

Continue until all burgers are cooked. It takes about 4 minutes for each side to get browned. Watch carefully, don't let the burgers burn adjust heat as needed.

Layer burgers on white paper towels in a plate as cooked.

For baking lentil burgers preheat oven to 400 degrees. Add 4 tablespoons of oil to the mix and mix in well. Wet pan lightly and line with parchment paper. Spray baking pan with non-stick spray. Use a large ice cream scooper sprayed with nonstick olive oil spray to scoop the burger mix and place into the pan. Flattened lightly and bake for 40 minutes until browned.

Preparation items: large bowl, large nonstick fry pan, nonstick oblong pan for baking, colander, stirring spoon, tablespoon, measuring cup and spoons, knife, flipper, cutting board, food processor, paper towels Parchment paper and medium pot.

Lima bean jambalaya

Serves: 12 Preparation Time: 10 minutes Cooking Time: 45 minutes Total Time 55 minutes:

Description: Very cheesy and taste great.

INGREDIENTS:

16 ounce pack of frozen lima beans rinsed

1 block firm organic sprouted tofu Rinsed, dried and cubed

1 onion rinsed and sliced

1 Large tomato

1 cup peeled and cubed red potatoes

1 teaspoon agave nectar

1 celery stalk rinsed sliced

1 cup shredded diaya dairy free cheese

2 organic carrots rinsed sliced

2 tablespoons Bragg's liquid amino

1 tablespoon grounded turmeric

1 teaspoon grounded paprika

1/4 teaspoon of cayenne pepper

1/2 teaspoon grounded thyme

1/2 teaspoon whole basil

3 fresh bay leaves

3 tablespoon olive oil

DIRECTIONS:

Preheat oven to 375 degree

Put tomato in a bowl and let sit in boiling hot water for 3 then poke and peel the skin off then slice.

Meanwhile put the frozen lima beans and tofu in large pot on top of the stove and cover. Steam the beans and tofu on medium heat for 20 minutes and drain off the liquid and pour the beans and tofu into a bowl.

Add the prepared slice carrots, tomatoes, onion, cubed potatoes and celery to the bowl.

Add the seasonings, bay leaves, 1/2 cup cheese and olive oil and stir lightly.

Pour bean mixture into a baking dish and sprinkle the remaining cheese on top and bake covered for 20 minutes. Uncover dish and bake for 5 minutes. Take out bay leaves and serve hot.

Preparation Items: large oven proof baking dish with lid, knife, large bowl, measuring cup and spoons, cutting board.

Lovely banana nut bread

Yield 2 loaves nut bread Preparation Time: 20 minutes Cooking Time: 45 minutes total time: 1 hour +5 minutes.

Description: moist and taste great anytime

INGREDIENTS:

3 cups organic spelt flour

1/2 cup coconut flour

1 teaspoon aluminum free baking soda

2 teaspoons aluminum free baking powder

1/4teaspoon sea salt

2 teaspoons grounded cinnamon

2 tablespoons grounded flaxseeds mixed with 6 tablespoons spring water

1/2 cup almond milk

1 tablespoon fresh lemon juice

1/2 cup vegan sour cream

2/3 cup grape seed oil

1 cup pure maple syrup

3 ripe bananas

2 teaspoon alcohol free vanilla flavor

1 cup walnut pieces

1 can organic nonstick olive oil spray

Topping (optional):

Mix together

1/4cup soft earth balance spread

1 tablespoon oatmeal

2 teaspoons vegan raw brown sugar

1 teaspoon cinnamon

1/4 cup chopped walnuts

DIRECTIONS:

Preheat oven to 350 degrees

Line nonstick pans with parchment paper and spray with olive oil nonstick spray and rub it all over the paper.

Mix together the grounded walnuts, sugar, oatmeal, margarine and cinnamon for the topping and set aside.

Mix the flaxseeds and water together and set aside

Mix milk and lemon juice together and let curdle

Sift together the dry ingredients into a large bowl then mix together with the whisker and set aside.

In the blender blend the grape seed oil, maple syrup, sour cream, and vanilla flavor.

Add the flaxseed mixture, bananas, milk and lemon mixture and blend well.

Then add the wet mixture to the dry ingredients adding a little at a time mixing with a spoon just enough to mix in everything.

Then fold in walnuts.

Pour evenly into prepared pans.

Sprinkle the topping on the top before baking.

Bake for 45 minutes then inserted long tooth pick in center to see if comes out clean. If uncooked batter is on tooth pick cook 3-4 minutes and test again.

Let bread cool before removing from pans to a plate and peeling off parchment paper.

Preparation items: food processor, large deep bowls and large Mixing spoon, 2 non-stick 4 x 8 loaf pans, measuring spoons and cups, long tooth picks.

Lovely vegan stir fry vegetables

Serves: 5 Preparation Time: 5 minutes Cooking Time: 10 minutes Total Time: 15 minutes

Description: Delicious mixture of vegetables that are colorful and taste great.

INGREDIENTS:

1 Indian eggplant

1 purple onion

1 yellow quash

2 zucchini squash

5 baby Bella mushrooms

1 medium purple onion

1/2 red bell pepper

1/2 block extra firm sprouted tofu rinsed well

2 tablespoon olive oil

1/4 teaspoon sea salt or to taste

1 teaspoon smoked paprika

1 teaspoon turmeric powder

DIRECTIONS:

Peel the mushroom rinse and sliced.

Wash all vegetables well then slice thin. Then add vegetables and mushrooms to non-stick pan. Add seasons, oil and turn heat to high to get started then turn to medium. Stir fry for a couple minutes then add the small cubed tofu and continue to stir fry for 10 minutes lightly mixing everything together. Turn off heat and continue to stir until the cooking process decrease. Serve over quinoa or yellow grits for breakfast.

Preparation items: cutting board, sharp knife, measuring spoons and cups, nonstick fry pan and rubber spatula

Luscious red velvet cake

Serves: 15 Preparation Time: 25 Cooking Time: 55 minutes. Total Time: 1 hour + 30 minutes

Description: Mellow red velvet cake with a hint of cocoa. This is a healthy cake and not overly sweet

INGREDIENTS:

1/2cup spelt flour

3cups unbleached unenriched all-purpose flour

2 teaspoons aluminum free baking powder

1 teaspoon aluminum free baking soda

1/4 teaspoon real sea salt

4 tablespoons well sifted organic beet powder

2 tablespoons Hershey's unsweetened cocoa powder

2 tablespoons grounded flaxseeds

6 tablespoons spring water

1 cup soft earth balance margarine

1/4 cup grape seed oil

2cups turbinino sugar

5.3 ounce container of silk vanilla soy yogurt

2-1/4cups almond milk with 2 tablespoon lemon juice and let curdle

2 teaspoons alcohol free vanilla flavor

1 cup crushed walnuts

Non-stick organic olive oil spray

DIRECTIONS:

Spray bundt cake pan well with nonstick olive oil spray and sprinkle a little flour around sides and bottom of pan and shake out excess flour or line round nonstick layer cake pans. Spray a little spray in the pan then line with parchment paper and spray lightly set aside. Preheat oven to 350 degrees.

In a large container sift the flours, baking powder baking soda, pre sifted beet powder, cocoa and the sea salt and whisk dry ingredients together very well.

With the blender, blend together the earth balance, grape seed oil, sugar and blend until well blended about 1/2 minute.

Then add milk and lemon juice mixture, flaxseed mixture, yogurt, flavor and continue mixing together in the blender for 2 seconds on low speed.

Next add the wet mixture a little at a time into the dry ingredients and mixing well with a large mixing spoon until all ingredients are blended in well then beat for 1 minute with electric mixer.

Pour the cake mixture into prepared bundt pan or two 9 inch cake pans and shake a little to even out the batter. Bake for 55 minutes for bundt cake. Inserted long tooth pick in center to see if comes out clean. If uncooked batter or crumbs is on tooth pick cook 3-4 minutes and test again. Allow cake to cool 10 minutes in the pan before inserting on a plate.

For layer cake bake for 35 minutes then inserted long tooth pick in center to see if comes out clean. If uncooked batter or crumbs is on tooth pick cook 3-4 minutes and test again. Allow cake to cool 10 minutes in the pan before inserting on a plate and removing parchment paper. Cool completely before frosting. Sprinkle crushed walnuts over the top of frosting.

Preparation items: non-stick bundt pan or 2- 9 inch non-stick layer cake pans, high speed blender, electric mixer measuring cups and spoons, mixing spoon, tooth picks, large spoon and large cake plates.

Mary's full-flavored creamy vinaigrette dressing

Yield 16 about ounces Preparation Time: 3 minutes blending Time 3
Total Time: 6 minutes

Description: I like to make my salad dressings from scratch so I can
control the sodium and use natural ingredients. This dressing has a
tangy sweet taste.

INGREDIENTS:

1 tablespoon mustard powder

1/8 teaspoon grounded turmeric

1/2 cup extra virgin olive oil

1 teaspoon dried basil

1 tablespoon grounded flax seeds

1 teaspoon celery seeds

Pinch of cayenne pepper

1/4 cup Bragg's apple cider vinegar

1 clove garlic peeled and rinsed

3 tablespoon light agave nectar

1 tablespoon Bragg's liquid amino- more if desired

1/2 cup spring water

DIRECTIONS:

Put all ingredients in a blender and blend 3 minutes or until well blended.

Dressing can be stored in refrigerator for 3 week. Shake well before using.

If dressing is too thick add a little spring water.

Moist lemon pound cake

Serves: 12 Preparation Time: 15 minutes Cooking Time: 40 minutes Total Time: 55 minutes

Description: Simply delicious and moist

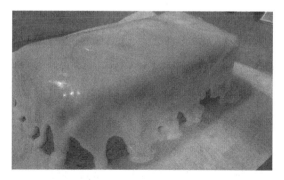

INGREDIENTS:

3-1/2cups basic homemade cake flour on page 285

2 teaspoons aluminum free baking powder

1 teaspoon aluminum free baking soda

1/4teaspoon real sea salt

1 cup soft earth balance buttery spread

1/3 cup olive oil

2 tablespoons light grounded flaxseeds mixed with 6 tablespoons spring water

1-1/2cups almond milk plus 2 tablespoons

3 teaspoons lemon juice

1 cup Easy homemade unsweetened apple sauce page 15

1-3/4cups vegan raw organic light brown cane sugar

Parchment paper

1 can organic non-stick olive oil spray

Preheat oven to 350 degrees.

DIRECTIONS:

Spray pan a little and line pans with parchment paper and spray lightly with olive oil set aside.

Sift the flour, baking soda, baking powder and salt into a large bowl.

In the blender mix the earth balance spread, oil, milk, raw sugar, lemon juice, flaxseed mixture and applesauce together until creamy.

Add the wet mixture to the flour mixture mixing well after each addition.

Continue using all of the wet mixture and mixing well

Scrape the sides of bowl and continue to mix just enough to blend everything together with electric mixer for 1 minute.

Pour the cake mixture into the prepared pans and shake the dish to even out the cake. Bake for 40 minutes then inserted long tooth pick in center to see if comes out clean. If uncooked batter or crumbs is on tooth pick cook 3-4 minutes and test again coked crumbs is okay.

Let the cake cool completely.

When cooled invert the cake to the plate and peel off parchment paper.

*Frosting of your choice or use tangy lemon frosting page 242
Decorate with ground lemon peel-optional

Preparation items needed: 2- 8x4 inch oblong nonstick loaf pans, measuring cups and spoons, whisker, electric mixer, large spoon, knife, large bowl and cutting board

My favorite vegan gingerbread cake

Serves 15: Preparation Time: 25 minutes Cooking Time 55 minutes
Total Time: 1hour-20 minutes

Description: Gingerbread is moist and taste great

I decided to make my own gingerbread cake. I came up with this
wonderful gingerbread cake.

INGREDIENTS:

3 -1/2cups spelt flour

2teaspoons aluminum free baking powder

1/2 teaspoon sea salt

1/2 teaspoon aluminum free baking soda

1 teaspoon ground nutmeg

2tablespoons ground ginger

2teaspoons ground cinnamon

1 cup earth balance buttery spread

1-3/4cups organic vegan raw brown sugar

1 tablespoon organic black molasses

2 teaspoon alcohol-free vanilla flavor

3/4cup almond milk

1/2cup vegan sour cream

2 tablespoon grounded flaxseeds mixed with 6 tbsp warm spring water

1 can organic non-stick olive oil spray

1 package parchment paper

DIRECTIONS:

Preheat oven to 350 degrees

Spray a rectangle baking pan with olive oil spray and line with parchment paper and spray a little with non-stick spray.

Mix the flaxseeds and water together and set aside.

*Have all ingredients room temperature.

Sift all dry ingredients into a large bowl and mix well.

Mix in food processor the earth balance, molasses, brown sugar, milk, sour cream, flaxseed mixture and mix until creamy.

Slowly add the wet mixture to the dry ingredients.

Mix with a mixing spoon until all ingredients are just blended in well.

Don't over mix.

Pour mixture into prepared pan and bake for 55 minutes then inserted long tooth pick in center to see if comes out clean. If uncooked batter or crumbs is on tooth pick cook 3-4 minutes and test again.

Let cake cool 10 minutes before removing from the pan and taking off parchment paper. Cool gingerbread completely before frosting.

Preparation items: heavy duty rectangle pan, measuring cups and spoons, food processor, sifter, stirring spoon and large bowls

Fantastic navy bean soup

Serves: 16 Preparation Time: 10 minutes Cooking Time: 1 hour Total Time: 1hour + 10 minutes

Description; Taste great and is healthy and easy to digest

This small white legume got its name from the US Navy they served it as a staple. Gluten free navy beans are very healthy and have goods protein, easy to digest and make a nice bean soup. Can be served with blue chips

INGREDIENTS:

2 pounds navy beans

3fresh carrots rinsed

1-large onion peeled and rinsed

6 cloves garlic peeled and rinsed

1-large red bell pepper cored rinsed

3 stalks of fresh celery rinsed

4 Roma tomatoes finely grounded

1/3 cup olive oil add last

1teaspoon grounded ginger or small piece fresh ginger

1/4teaspoon cayenne pepper or more if desired

1 teaspoon dark agave nectar add last

1 tablespoon dried whole grounded sage

1 tablespoon grounded thyme

1 teaspoon sea salt or to taste add last

1/ 2 teaspoon aluminum free baking soda for soaking beans

2 gallon spring water

DIRECTIONS:

Pick small stones and debris then soak navy beans overnight in spring water and baking soda. Quick soak follow directions on bag

Rinse beans well in spring water before cooking.

Cut the carrots, garlic, red bell pepper, tomatoes and celery in halves and grind fine.

Put the prepared veggies, oil, sage, thyme, cayenne pepper, ginger and navy beans into the pot and sauté for 10 minutes and stir often.

Add 5 cups of water and bring bean mixture to a boil uncovered on top of the stove.

Stir beans and reduce heat to medium/low covered pot and cook 1hour and 20 minutes or until the beans are tender add more water as needed.

Take out ginger root and put portions of the cooked beans and veggies in a food processor with 1/3cup water for each portion of beans and blend until creamy continue until all of the beans are blended. There will be about 3 portions of beans to be blended.

Pour the blended beans into a large pot and rinse out food processor with 1/2cup water and add to the pot.

Add the salt, maple syrup, tomato ketchup and stir in well and simmer on low heat for 15 minutes.

Option: Some of the beans can be left whole if desired.

Taste and add more seasoning and water if needed and stir.

To warm place bean soup pot into another pot filled 1/3 with water to heat before serving.

Left over soup can be frozen.

Preparation items: large stainless steel heavy duty pot, large stirring spoon, chopping board, knife, food processor, measuring spoons and cups.

Out of sight vegan chocolate chip cookies

Yield 3 dozen cookies Preparation Time15 minutes Cooking Time: 10 minutes for each dozen Total Time: 25 minutes

Recipe Description: Chocolate and soft and very good. Chocolate lovers will have a feast on these cookies. These were made with sugar.

INGREDIENTS:

2-1/2cups spelt flour

1/2 teaspoon aluminum free baking powder

1 teaspoon aluminum free baking soda

1/2cup dark Hershey unsweetened cocoa

1/4 teaspoon sea salt

2 tablespoons grounded flax seeds mixed in 4 tablespoons warm spring water

1-1/2 cups turbinado sugar in the raw

1/2cup almond milk

1/2cup olive oil

1 teaspoons alcohol free real vanilla flavor

1 cup vegan carob chips or vegan chocolate chips

2 tablespoons pumpkin seeds

1 cup walnut pieces

Parchment paper

Organic non-stick olive oil

DIRECTIONS:

Preheat oven 375 degrees

Cover cookie sheet with parchment paper and spray lightly parchment paper.

Coarsely ground the pumpkin seeds in food processor.

Chop the walnuts into small pieces.

Put the flour, sea salt, baking soda, baking powder, cocoa and pumpkin seeds, walnuts and carob chips in a bowl, stir well.

Put olive oil, flavor, milk, sugar, flaxseed mixture in blender and blend well.

Then add the wet mixture to the flour mixture and mix with a large spoon until everything is moist and mixed.

Drop a small scooper or a tablespoon full of cookie dough onto the cookie sheet and press lightly with plastic cup sprayed with nonstick spray. Or if possible the dough can be roll with hands in medium balls then press down lightly.

Space the cookies apart.

Bake 10 minutes

Let cookies cool for 5 minutes then remove from parchment paper.

Use wax paper between each layer of cookies to prevent them from sticking together. Place cookies in covered container when cooled.

Preparation items: large bowl, cookie sheets, parchment paper, measuring cups and spoons, blender, small cookie scooper, tablespoon, wax paper

Note: 1 cup agave nectar and no milk can be substituted for the sugar in the recipe or 1 cup stevia in the raw + 1/2 cup turbinado sugar in the raw can be used to cut down on the sugar content in the recipe.

***This mixture can be made into brownies, just flatten with a plastic cup and bake for 25 minutes or until toothpick comes out clean.

Quick carrot cake

Serves: 12 Preparation Time: 10 minutes Cooking Time: 45 minutes
Total Time: 55 minutes

Description: Very mellow and the pineapple, and nuts complements the cake.

INGREDIENTS:

1-1/3 cups pure maple syrup

1/3 cup almond milk

2-1/2 cups spelt flour

2 teaspoons aluminum free baking powder

1/2teaspoon aluminum free baking soda

2 teaspoon alcohol free vanilla flavor

2/3 cup soft earth balance spread

2 tablespoon flaxseeds mixed with

4 tablespoon warm spring water

2 large cleaned carrots ends cut off and carrots cut in pieces

1/3 cup vegan sour cream

1/4 cup fresh crushed pineapple drained well

1-1/4cups walnut pieces

1 package parchment paper

Non-stick organic olive oil spray

DIRECTIONS:

Preheat oven to 350 degrees

Line baking pan with parchment paper and spray lightly with olive oil nonstick spray.

Mix flaxseeds together with the water and set aside.

Chop walnuts in food processor.

Grind carrots in food processor very fine.

Wisk dry ingredients and raisins together well with the flour and set aside.

Put the maple syrup, oil, flaxseed mixture, milk, flavor and sour cream in a blender and blend well. Add the carrots and pineapple and blend well.

Pour the wet mixture slowly into the dry ingredient and mix well with large spoon.

Fold in the nuts.

Pour the batter into prepared pan. Bake for 45 minutes then inserted long tooth pick in center to see if comes out clean. If uncooked batter or crumbs is on tooth pick cook 3-4 minutes and test again.

Preparation items: 1 medium oblong baking pan, measuring cups and spoons, mixing spoon, large mixing spoon, heavy duty blender food processor and large bowl.

Raw creamy red bell pepper salad dressing

Yields 1 pint Preparation Time: 5 minutes blending Time 3 minutes
Total Time: 8 minutes

Description: delicious on any salad or use as a marinade.

INGREDIENTS:

1 fresh garlic peeled rinsed

Small piece of purple onion

1/2 medium red bell pepper cored and rinsed

1/2cup extra virgin olive oil

3 tablespoons pure maple syrup

1/4 tablespoon Bragg's apple cider vinegar

1 teaspoon grounded paprika

1/3 teaspoon sea salt

1/2cup pumpkin seeds

2 tablespoons grounded flax seeds

1/2cup spring water

DIRECTIONS:

Wash and clean all vegetables, dry off excess water and put them in the blender.

Blend for 3 minute on high speed or until all veggies are ground and the texture is creamy.

Taste and add more seasoning and some of the water if needed.

Rinse out the blender with part of the remaining water and pour into the container of salad dressing.

Shake well and store into the refrigerator. If too thick add a little spring water

Preparation items needed: measuring cup and spoons, high speed blender, air tight container, cutting board and sharp knife.

Raw supreme carrot "mock tuna" salad

Serves: 10 Preparation Time: 18 minutes mixing Time 15 minutes Total Time: 33 minutes.

Description: I was looking for another way to use the pulp when I juiced carrots. So I tried mixing some seasoning added ground veggies to the carrot pulp and it turned out nice and very tasty so we use this recipe to make a quick meal on weekends. This raw carrot salad is so versatile. It can be placed on top of a tossed salad, placed on crackers as an appetizer or make a sandwich. It's awesome! We love it.

The carrot juice is a refreshing and a healthy drink.

INGREDIENTS:

20 fresh unpeeled carrots washed, ends cut off and dried

1/4cup of fresh onions peeled and rinsed

1 fresh red bell pepper rinsed and cored

2 stalks of fresh celery rinsed and chopped

1 fresh clove garlic peeled and rinsed

3/4cup organic sweet pickle relish drained before adding to salad

1 tablespoon organic agave nectar and 1 small peeled Fuji apple

1 quart Follow your heart vegenaise spread

2 tablespoons ground flax seeds

1 teaspoon ground paprika

1/2 teaspoon cilantro

1/4 teaspoon kelp- optional

1/8 teaspoon cayenne pepper optional

1/3teaspoon real sea salt or1tablespoon Bragg's liquid amino or to taste

DIRECTIONS:

Put all fresh cleaned veggies except carrots in food processor and coarsely chop then drained and set aside.

Chop apple in food processor very fine, set aside

Before juicing the carrots in juicer place the pulp catcher and the juice catcher in place then began juicing.

In a large bowl empty the carrot pulp, the ground veggies, chopped apple and dry seasonings and mix well.

(Save the carrot juice to drink.)

Add liquid amino, relish, agave nectar, sandwich spread and mix thoroughly.

Taste and add more seasoning and spread if needed.

Sprinkle a little paprika over the top of the carrot salad

*To make sandwiches put leaves of romaine lettuce on a slice of whole wheat bread.

Spread the carrot salad on top of the lettuce and top with slices of tomato and alfalfa sprouts then put spread on top slice of bread and place on top of sandwiches and enjoy!

Preparation items: heavy duty juicer with pulp and juice catcher, large bowl, sharp knife, colander, measuring spoons and cups, cutting board, large spoon

Red Swiss chard & no cheese sauce

Serves: 4 Preparation Time: 5 minutes Cooking Time: 8 minutes

Total Time: 13 minutes

Description: This is a colorful and healthy dish that looks good with the cheese sauce sprinkled with paprika

INGREDIENTS:

2bunches red Swiss chard

1/8 teaspoon sea salt

1/4 teaspoon garlic powder

1/8 teaspoon cayenne pepper

2 tablespoon extra olive oil

1/2teaspoon paprika add last

DIRECTIONS:

Clean and wash the Swiss chard thoroughly in spring water then slice.

Drain Swiss chard in salad spinner

Put the washed and drained Swiss chard in a medium size pot.

Add the seasonings and stir to mix together. Steam covered for 8 minutes on medium low heat.

**Make sure the Swiss chard is well drained before adding the cheese sauce and sprinkle paprika on the top.

Serve warm.

No cheese sauce

Preparation items needed: medium stainless steel heavy duty pot, stirring spoons, measuring spoons and cups, cutting board, large deep colander.

Ridge Gourd (Chinese okra) Stir fry

Serves: 6 Preparation Time: 15minutes Cooking Time: 20 minutes. Total Time35 minutes

Description: This is a very delicious dish and it is easy to cook. It is a loveable vegetable.

INGREDIENTS:

6 Ridge Gourds (Chinese okra)

2 medium red potatoes washed and sliced in small cubes

2 Roma tomatoes washed and sliced

1 medium purple onion washed and sliced thin

1 teaspoon chili powder

1 teaspoon grounded turmeric

1 teaspoon real sea salt add last

1/8 teaspoon ground ginger

1 tablespoon paprika powder

1 tablespoon grounded masala seasoning

1 pinch cayenne pepper

3 tablespoons olive oil

DIRECTIONS:

Soak gourds in aluminum free baking soda and water for 5 minutes then scraped the ridges off but leave the green skin on.

Prepare the vegetables.

Rinse and dry the gourds well then cut lengthwise then cubed in medium pieces and take out the seeds if hard.

Put cubed gourds into warm oil and then turn heat on top of stove to high to start the cooking process when gourds start to cook stir and turn heat to medium.

Stir fry the gourds for 5 minutes add the onions, seasonings and sliced potatoes and continue stir frying for 15 minutes.

Add the tomatoes and sea salt and continue cooking uncovered on low heat until all liquid is gone takes about 5 minutes.

Serve warm.

Preparation item: large heavy duty pan, cutting board, knife, large colander and large stirring spoons, measuring cups and spoons, large deep basin.

Rosemary pinto bean burgers

Yield about 8 burgers Preparation Time: 25 minutes Cooking Time 35 minute. Total time 60 minutes

Description: These burgers smell and taste great. they cook up very nice and make a nice meat substitute I always cook up lots beans and freeze them so I will always have them on hand. The burgers in the picture are fried.

INGREDIENTS:

2 cups cooked drained pinto beans

1/2 peeled and rinsed onion chopped fine in food processor and 1/2 chopped small with the knife

1/2 red bell pepper rinsed and cored

1 stalk celery, washed well

Small piece of fresh ginger peeled and rinsed

1 teaspoon dried cilantro

1 tablespoon garlic powder

3 tablespoons Bragg's liquid amino

Pinch of red pepper seeds

1 sprig of fresh rosemary, use leaves only

1 teaspoon fennel seeds

1-1/2 cups raw cashews

1-1/2 cups couscous page 56

2 tablespoon ground flax seeds

6 tablespoons bean liquid or water

1/2 cup olive oil

Paper towels

Parchment paper

DIRECTIONS:

Cooking the beans:

First, pick out any small rocks or debris then soak in spring water and 1 tsp aluminum free baking soda overnight then drain and rinse well. For quick cook follow directions on bag. Sauté the pinto beans uncovered in 1 cup water and small piece of ginger on high heat to boil then turn heat to medium and add 5 cups water and cook for 2 hours covered or until tender then drain off the liquid and measure out 2 cups and proceed to make burgers.

Grind the prepared onion, rosemary leaves, celery, red bell pepper and fennel seeds coarsely in food processor.

Grind cashews to a course meal.

Put the beans and flaxseed mixture in the food processor and crush the beans.

197

Sauté the vegetables for 2 minutes in 1 tablespoon of oil

Add all seasonings, sautéed veggies, cashews, couscous and liquid amino to the bowl.

Mix everything together well.

The mixture should be medium stiff if too stiff add a little bean liquid to the mix and mix well.

Put a large nonstick fry pan on burner on top of the stove and put 4 tablespoons of the oil in pan.

Turn the heat to medium.

Scoop the burger mix with an ice cream scooper sprayed with non-stick spray and place burgers in the pan and cook for 4 minutes then flip over with a flipper and flatten lightly with the flipper and cook for 4 minutes. Make sure they are browned on both sides before removing from the pan. Add oil as needed.

These burgers can be baked if desired.

Preheated oven to 400 degrees

Line pan with parchment paper and spray with nonstick spray.

Add the 1/4 cup oil to the burger mix and mix in well. Scoop the burger mix with an ice cream scooper sprayed with non-stick spray and place burgers in the pan. Flatten lightly with flipper sprayed lightly with nonstick spray Bake burgers uncovered for 40 minutes. Turn the broiler on and lightly brown the tops if needed. Watch carefully so they don't burn.

Preparation items: 1 plate, white paper towels, large bowl, measuring cup and spoons, cutting board, food processor flipper and large nonstick fry pan, baking pan and parchment paper.

Savory chunky tomato pasta sauce

Serves: 10 Preparation Time: 15 minutes Cooking Time: 55 minutes
Total Time: 1hour + 10 minutes

Description: very delicious and the sauce gets better the next day

I came up with this recipe after making my meet sauce and talking to
my son who thought I should have a vegetable pasta sauces and lo this
is savory sauce that I and the creator has created.

INGREDIENTS:

4 Cloves garlic peeled rinsed and chopped

1 onion peeled rinsed cubed

1 cup baby Bella mushrooms rinsed and sliced

2 large fresh Roma tomatoes rinsed skinned and chopped

1red bell pepper cored rinsed

1 stalk celery

1 zucchini squash

1 tablespoon basil

1 tablespoon oregano

1 tablespoon dried cilantro or 3 pieces of fresh cilantro

1/8 teaspoon cayenne pepper to taste

1 tablespoon grounded paprika

5 tablespoon cold pressed olive oil

1-24 oz jar Rega gluten free organic tomato puree

2 small can Muir organic tomato paste mixed with 2 cup spring water

2 tablespoons pure maple syrup

1 teaspoon sea salt or to taste

1/2gallon spring water

DIRECTIONS:

Soak the tomatoes in boiling water for 3 minutes poke small holes in tomato to remove the skin and chop chunky.

Rinse mushrooms then slice the cleaned mushrooms

Cube the zucchini squash into medium pieces

Chop well the garlic, onion and celery in the food processor

Put the sliced mushrooms, garlic, onion, celery and all of the dry seasonings to the heavy duty deep electric pan or medium deep pot with 5 tablespoons olive oil and sauté on medium heat on top of the stove for 3 minutes.

Stir often and watch carefully so nothing will burn. Mix in tomato puree, tomato paste and water mixture and stir well.

Cook covered on medium/low heat for 40 minutes stirring often.

Taste and add prepared red peppers, zucchini squash, tomatoes, maple syrup and more seasonings if needed. Stir and cook for 10 minutes more.

Serve over your favorite organic pasta.

Vegan parmesan cheese can be sprinkled over pasta.

Preparation items needed: 1-large heavy duty stainless steel electric skillet or heavy duty pot, measuring spoons and 3 measuring cup, large wooden stirring spoons, can opener, medium bowl, large bowl and knife.

Savory collard and mustard greens with turnip roots

Serves: 12 Preparation Time: 20 minutes Cooking Time: 55 minutes Total Time: 1hr +15minutes

This dish is a family favorite and they go perfect with the cream of wheat bread page 272.

INGREDIENTS:

2 bunches organic mustard greens

2 bunches organic collard greens

2 large organic turnip roots cut in medium size cubes and *add last)

1 tablespoon Bragg's apple cider vinegar

1/4 cup extra virgin cold pressed olive oil

1 teaspoon sea salt

1 small onion peeled and washed

1 teaspoon garlic powder

1/4 teaspoon Cayenne pepper

1/2 cup spring water

1 tablespoon pure maple syrup- optional

1 teaspoon paprika reserved for last

DIRECTIONS:

Put the onion in food processor and grind fine.

Clean and wash collards and mustard greens thoroughly then drain off the water from the greens and slice them thinly.

Cut turnip roots in medium cubes wash well. Set aside.

Put cleaned and drained greens in a large pot, add the water and onions, all of the seasonings.

Stir to mix all together and cook on high heat on top of the stove until the greens began to boil.

Then turn heat to medium and cook for 40 minutes. If needed, add 1/2 cup spring water.

Add the agave nectar and stir in thoroughly.

Add the turnip roots and sprinkle the reserved paprika and salt over the roots and continue to cook for 15 minutes more or until a fork can be easily inserted into the roots.

Add the oil and mix the greens and turnip roots together.

Sprinkle a little paprika over visible turnip root Serve warm.

Preparation item: large heavy duty pot with lid, cutting board food processor stainless steel pot with lid, large colander and large stirring spoons, measuring cups and spoons, large deep basin, sharp knife.

Savory meatless meatloaf

Serves: 8 Preparation Time: 15 minutes Cooking Time: 1hour 40 minutes: total Time 1hr 55 minutes

Description: this meat loaf is savory and delicious also make a beautiful showing. This meat loaf can be sliced and served with stone ground mustard and ketchup. Always soak enough for freezing.

INGREDIENTS:

4 cups of presoaked textured vegetable protein granules

1/2cup spelt flour

3 Slices spelt bread toasted

1 cup raw sunflower seeds

1 large onion peeled rinsed and chopped

1 red bell pepper rinsed and chopped

4 cloves of garlic, peeled rinsed

1/3 cup olive oil (reserve 1 tablespoon

1/4cup Bragg's liquid amino (reserve 1 tablespoon)

3 tablespoons paprika

1 tablespoon grounded fennel

2 teaspoons fennel seeds

1 tablespoon ground cilantro

1/2teaspoon red pepper seeds

2 tablespoons grounded flaxseeds

1/4 cup almond milk

1 cup shredded vegan cheese

1can organic olive oil spray

For basting:

Reserved 1 tablespoon

Reserved 1 tablespoon

1 drop gravy master

3/4 cup of hot spring water

DIRECTIONS:

Preheat oven to 375 degrees

Spray baking dish with olive oil spray

Soak protein overnight in spring water or for 30 minutes in hot water and squeeze the water out before using or freezing.

Reserve 4 cups of protein.

Chop garlic, onions and bell pepper in food processor.

Finely grind sunflower seeds in food processor.

Finely grind spelt bread.

Put all of the above ingredients in a large bowl.

Dump the protein mixture in into prepared baking dish and shape with your hands into a loaf.

+ For basting: heat water and mix with reserved olive oil, liquid amino and 1 small drop of gravy master.

Pour half over the loaf and keep the rest warm.

Bake covered for 1hour.

Take the loaf out of oven and pour the remaining hot water mixture over the loaf.

Bake uncovered for 30 minutes until the top is browned and feel firm. Sprinkle the cheese over the loaf and cook until cheese is melted.

Let loaf sit on cooling board for 10 minutes before serving.

Preparation items needed: Large baking dish, sharp knife, measuring cups and spoons, cutting board, food processor and large bowl.

Savory turkey-less dressing

Serves: 10 Preparation Time: 10 minutes Cooking Time: 35 minutes Total Time: 45 minutes

Description: Turkey-less dressing cook-up very lovely and the taste is very flavorful.

This is our family favorite for thanksgiving

INGREDIENTS:

Large pan of cooked cream of wheat bread

4 cups vegetable broth page 259

4 tablespoons fresh grounded sage

1/3 teaspoons cayenne pepper

1 teaspoon turmeric powder

1 cup fresh sliced mushrooms

2 garlic cloves peeled, rinsed

1 medium onion peeled and rinsed

1 carrot rinsed ends cut off

2 stalks celery rinsed

1/3 cup Powered chick less broth mix

3 tablespoons Bragg's liquid amino or to taste

1/4 cup raisins (optional)

3 tablespoon earth balance buttery spread

2 teaspoon of maple syrup

1 golden or red delicious apple

DIRECTIONS:

Preheat oven to 400 degrees

Grind garlic, carrot, celery and onion in the food processor.

Chop fine peeled and cored apple in food processor.

Sauté prepared mushrooms and vegetables in the earth balance spread for 2 minutes.

Crumble the cream of wheat bread in a large bowl.

Mix in 1 cup of broth at a time, mashing the crumble bread with a potato masher.

Continue mixing in the vegetable broth until the mixture is coarsely loose.

Add sautéed vegetables, broth powder and raisins.

Add all of the seasonings, maple syrup and liquid amino, finely chopped apple and mix thoroughly.

Taste and add more seasonings if needed.

Pour the dressing into the prepared pan.

Bake uncovered for 35 minutes or until golden brown.

Tofu no turkey breast

Vegetable broth

Cream of wheat bread

Preparation items needed: large bowl, measuring spoons and cups and potato masher, 10"x15" stainless steel baking pan, sauté pan and food processor, mixing spoon, cutting board and sharp knife.

Scrumptious curried tofu

Serves: 6 Preparation Time: 10 minutes Cooking Time: 43minutes
Total Time: 53 minutes

Description: Curried tofu with lots of flavor and color

INGREDIENTS:

2 packs extra firm tofu rinsed and cut in medium cubed

1 medium onion peeled rinsed

1 stalk of fresh celery rinsed

1 red bell pepper rinsed and cored

3 garlic cloves peeled rinsed

1 teaspoon paprika powder

1/8 teaspoon cayenne pepper powder

1 tablespoon turmeric powder

2 tablespoons Jamaican curry powder or enough to coat tofu

1/2 teaspoon thyme

1 teaspoon ground ginger

3 tablespoons Bragg's liquid amino

1/3 cup organic olive oil

1-1/2 cups spring water

DIRECTIONS:

Put garlic, bell pepper, celery and onion in food processor and chop.

Sauté the vegetables in oil for 5 minutes

Put the prepared tofu in a gallon size plastic bag along with all of the dry seasonings.

Gently shake to mix well and transfer tofu to the sautéed vegetables. Pour the amino over the tofu, and gently toss tofu and vegetables together.

Cook on medium heat for 8 minutes tossing occasionally.

Add water and continue to simmer covered on medium/ low heat for 30 minutes.

Taste and add more seasoning if desired and water and cook a few minutes. Sprinkle paprika on top of finish dish. Serve over long grain basmati rice

Preparation items needed: large nonstick sauté pan, food processor, stirring spoon, measuring spoons and cup, knife and cutting board.

Variety: Sometimes I add mushrooms to the sautéed vegetable pan.

*If desired: to thicken, mix 1 teaspoon potato starch with 2 tablespoons water and add in the last 10 minutes of cook time

Smooth vegan cheesy sauce

Yield: 1 pint Preparation Time: 10 minutes Cooking Time: 10 minutes
Total Time: 20 minutes

Description: This cheesy sauce is smooth and taste wonderful and the
vegan cheese melts.

Cheesy sauce is delicious wherever the imagination calls for a cheese
sauce or dip.

INGREDIENTS:

1 block vegan daiya cheddar cheese

3/4cup nutritional yeast

3 cups almond milk

1/3 teaspoon turmeric

1 tablespoon powdered potato starch

Dash of cayenne pepper

2 tablespoons earth balance buttery spread

1/2 teaspoon sea salt

DIRECTIONS:

211

Chop cheese very fine in food processor and set aside.

Melt earth balance buttery spread in a medium pot on low heat on top of the stove.

Put the turmeric, yeast, potato starch, cayenne pepper and sea salt in a large measuring cup and add milk and stir well with a large spoon and when the mixture is smooth add to the pot. Add the grounded cheese and continue to cook on medium heat stirring constantly with the whisker until the cheese is completely melted and the sauce is creamy.

Preparation items needed: medium stainless steel pot, food processor, measuring spoons and cups, stainless steel whisker or large wooden spoon.

Southern fried sweet corn

Serves: 10 Preparation Time: 10minutes Cooking Time: 20 minutes
Total Time: 30 minutes

Description: This will take you back to the days mother would cook fresh corn cut off the cob. Is a yummy delicious vegan style fried corn

INGREDIENTS:

10 ears of fresh corn husked and rinsed

1 teaspoon sea salt

1/2teaspoon raw organic vegan sugar optional

1/2teaspoon cinnamon

1/2 fresh red bell pepper cored rinsed and chopped fine

1 small fresh onion peeled rinsed and chopped fine

2 fresh cloves garlic peeled rinsed and chopped fine

1/8 teaspoon cayenne

1/3 stick vegan margarine

2 tablespoons organic potato starch mixed with 1/3 cup of spring water.

DIRECTIONS:

Prepare the vegetables and set aside.

Cut the corn off the cob and scrap the cob with the knife into the deep bowl.

Put the earth balance spread into a large heavy-duty fry pan to get hot then put the corn, prepared vegetables, cinnamon and sea salt into the pan with the corn.

Stir to mix everything together. Fry on medium heat for 15 minutes.

Add the sugar and cook for 5 minutes or until most of the liquid is absorbed and the corn starts to brown.

Taste and adjust seasoning if needed. Serve hot.

Preparation items needed: large heavy-duty stainless steel fry pan, measuring cup and spoons, sharp knife, cutting board and large bowl.

Southern style smothered tofu

Serves: 12 Preparation Time: 15 minutes Cooking Time: 45 minutes
Total Time: 60 minutes

Description: This dish is excellent meat substitute and very delicious.

INGREDIENTS:

2 packs extra firm organic tofu rinsed and dried

1/2piece off onion rinse, peel sliced thin

1 stalk fresh celery washed, sliced thin

2 cloves garlic peeled, rinsed slice thin

1 teaspoon whole dry basil

1/2teaspoon grounded ginger

1/4 teaspoon of cayenne pepper

4tablespoons grounded turmeric

6 tablespoons cold pressed olive oil

3tablespoons Bragg's liquid amino

2 large organic tomatoes

1quart spring water

DIRECTIONS:

Put the tomato in two cups of boiling hot water and let them sit for 3 minutes then peel and cubed.

Prepare the vegetables and set aside.

Rinse and dry the tofu with a paper towel before slicing each package into 6 slices.

Marinate slices in the liquid amino for 15 minutes.

Meanwhile mix the dry seasonings together in a large plate then after marinating tofu lay the tofu slices in the mixture and coat both sides. Heat a large fry pan with 4 tablespoons of olive oil on medium heat and place 4 slices of tofu at a time into the hot oil and brown well on both sides.

Add olive oil as needed until all of the tofu slices is browned.

Once browned place the slices on a clean plate and set aside.

Wash the fry pan and Sauté all prepared veggies and cubed tomatoes with 2 table oil for 2 minutes. Then pour the remaining leftover liquid amino out of plate into pan with veggies and sauté for another minute and then pour into a bowl.

Use brown gravy to make the gravy.

Then add the veggies to the gravy and stir.

Add cooked tofu slices and cook uncovered on medium heat until start to boil then reduce to low and simmer covered for 10 minute and sprinkle paprika on top. Serve over nutty flavored quinoa or long grain basmati brown rice

Preparation item needed: large size non- stick stainless fry pan measuring cups and spoons, knife, 2-large plate and bowl.

Spicy protein sausage patties

Yield 12 patties Preparation Time: 25 minute Cooking Time: 30 minutes Total Time: 55 minutes

Soak protein overnight in a bowl or for 30 minutes in boiling hot water. Squeeze out the water before using in recipe.

Description: These patties are so versatile and taste so good they can be eaten at breakfast or dinner.

INGREDIENTS:

3-1/2cups presoaked textured vegetable protein granules

4 tablespoons grounded sage

1/2 teaspoon red pepper seeds

1 tablespoon grounded flaxseeds

1 teaspoon grounded thyme

1 tablespoons fennel grounded

1 tablespoon fennel seeds

1 tablespoon vegan turbinino sugar in the raw

1 teaspoon grounded nutmeg

3 tablespoons Bragg's liquid amino

2/3 cup spelt flour

1 cup raw cashews

1/2 fresh onions peeled rinsed

1/2 piece fresh red bell pepper cored rinsed

2 garlic cloves peeled rinsed

1/2cup extra virgin olive oil

DIRECTIONS:

Grind garlic, onion and red bell pepper in food processor very fine

Sauté the vegetables in 2 tablespoons of the oil and set aside

Finely grind sunflower seeds in the food processor.

Put all ingredients and sautéed vegetables and 2 tablespoons of the olive oil in a large bowl and mix well.

Place 4 tablespoons of olive oil in a large non-stick fry pan and let oil get warm on medium heat on top of the stove.

Shape and flatten patties with hands and place 4 patties in the pan and let brown takes 4 minutes for each side to brown. If needed flip patties again and cook until nice and brown.

Continue cooking 4 patties each time by adding olive oil as needed to the fry pan until all of the patties are cooked.

Place on serving plate lined with paper towels to drain and serve warm Preheat oven to 400 degrees.

These patties can be baked. But mix 4 tablespoons olive oil in the mixture. Spray the pan well with nonstick spray. Bake for 40 minutes. Let patties rest for 5 minutes before serving.

Prep items: large nonstick frying pan, plastic flipper and large bowl, measuring spoons, cups, food processor, cutting board and sharp knife, baking pan, paper towels

Spicy vegan black bean soup

Serves: 8 Preparation Time: 11 minutes cooking time: 1hour + 35 minutes Total time: 1hr +46 minutes

Description: I garnished the soup with sautéed tofu, slice of roma tomato and bits of romaine

This black bean soup is great anytime and it is easy to make.

INGREDIENTS:

3cups dried black beans

1 onion peeled rinsed and chopped

4cloves garlic peeled rinsed and chopped

1/2large red bell pepper washed cored and chopped

1 tomato rinsed and chopped

1 stalk celery rinsed and chopped

1 tablespoon grounded turmeric

1 teaspoon grounded thyme

1/2 teaspoon grounded ginger

1 tablespoon ground cumin

1/8 teaspoon ground cayenne pepper or more

1 tablespoon olive oil

1 teaspoon pure maple syrup

1/2 teaspoon sea salt

8 cups spring water

1 teaspoon aluminum free baking soda

DIRECTIONS:

Look for any debris before soaking the beans.

Soak the beans overnight in a bowl of water and 1 tsp aluminum free baking soda. For quick soak follow directions on bag.

Chop the veggies very fine in the food processor.

Rinse the beans well in spring water and drain.

Then put them in large pot along with all the seasonings, ground veggies and sauté for 10 minutes on medium heat.

Then start the cooking process on top of the stove on high heat until the beans began to boil then turn heat to medium/low and cover pot and continue to cook for 1-1/2 hours or until beans are tender. Add water as needed. When the beans are done take out 1 cup of beans and put in blender with1 cup spring water and puree then and them put back into the soup pot. If the soup is too thick add a cup of spring water. Stir and cook for 5 minutes.

Add the olive oil, salt and stir. Garnish with sautéed tofu, pieces of lettuce and red bell peppers

Serve warm.

For variety: after pureeing the beans add 1/3 cup cooked millet to the pot and simmering for 10 minutes.

Preparation items: large heavy duty stainless steel pot, cutting board, food processor, measuring cup and spoons

Spicy vegetable gravy

Serves: 6 Preparation Time: 5 minutes Cooking Time: 23 minutes Total Time: 28 minutes

Description: This gravy is spicy and delightful colorful and can be used wherever gravy is needed

INGREDIENTS:

1-stalk celery rinsed and sliced

1-purple onion peeled rinsed sliced

1-garlic chopped fine

3-roma tomatoes skinned and cut in quarters

1 small piece of zucchini and cut in small quarters

1 small piece of red bell pepper chopped small

3 tablespoons liquid amino

1-1/2 tablespoons grape seed oil

2cups spring water

1 teaspoon cilantro

1tabspoon paprika powder

1 tiny pinch red pepper seeds

1/2 tablespoon turmeric powder

1 tablespoon potato starch mixed with 1/3 cup spring water add last

DIRECTIONS:

Place tomatoes in a bowl of boiling hot water for 3 minutes then peel it and cube them.

Chop garlic and onion in food processor and slice and quarter the other vegetables.

Put the prepared celery, zucchini, onion, garlic, bell pepper and seasonings into a large sauté pan and sauté them in the grape seed oil for 3 minutes on medium heat on top of the stove.

Add the chopped tomatoes, liquid amino and 2 cups of water to the pan and let it began to boil then whisk in the potato starch mixture whisking constantly.

Continue cooking on medium low heat for 20 minutes; whisking gently occasionally.

Taste and adjust seasoning as desired.

Serve over long grain basmati brown rice

Preparation items needed: large no-stick sauté pan, chopping board, sharp knife, measuring spoons and cups, large stirring spoon. Food processor

Jazzy steamed cabbage

Serves: 8 Preparation Time: 10 Cooking Time: 25 minutes Total Time: 35 minutes

Description: This cabbage is crunchy, colorful and taste great

Cabbage is healthy and has lots of vitamins.

INGREDIENTS:

1 Medium head of fresh cabbage

1small fresh onions

1/2 fresh red bell pepper

2fresh carrots, sliced

1 teaspoon sea salt optional

1 small jalapeño pepper deseeded, washed and sliced

1 tablespoon sliced almonds

1/8 teaspoon Basil flakes

1 teaspoon garlic powder

3 tablespoons olive oil

DIRECTIONS:

Slice all veggies and cabbage medium fine and wash them thoroughly.

Put the cabbage and veggies in a large colander to drain off all excess water.

Now put the cabbage in a large pot and add the almonds, earth balance spread, seasonings and basil flakes.

Stir well to mix everything together.

Let the cabbage come to a quick boil on high heat stirring constantly then steam the cabbage for 25 minutes on medium heat. Add the oil and stir well.

Serve hot as a side dish.

Preparation items needed: large stainless steel pot, knife, stirring spoon, cutting board, measuring spoons and cups and large colander.

Steamed kale and carrots

Serves: 8 Preparation Time: 10 minutes Cooking Time: 25 minutes
Total Time: 35 minutes

Description: Kale and carrots are steam lightly to preserve their
vitamins. This is a healthy delicious dish.

INGREDIENTS:

3 organic carrots washed and sliced

2 bunches of fresh organic kale soaked and washed whole then drained
and sliced

1/2 onions peeled rinsed and chopped

1 teaspoon garlic powder

1/2teaspoon sea salt optional

1/8 teaspoon cayenne pepper

3 tablespoons grape seed oil add last

DIRECTIONS:

Soak and wash whole kale thoroughly and put in a large colander to
drain off excess water then slice.

225

Wash and slice the carrots and chop the rinsed onion.

Put the prepared kale and carrots in a large pot along with all of seasonings and finely chopped onions.

Steam the veggies on medium heat for 25 minutes stirring occasionally. Add oil and stir serve hot.

Preparation items needed: large heavy-duty stainless steel pot, measuring cup and spoons, chopping board, sharp knife and large colander.

Steamed savory purple cabbage and plantains

Serves: 8 Preparation Time: 10 minutes Cooking Time: 20 minutes
        Total Time: 30 minutes

Description: Beautiful and savory dish that is an excellent side dish and gluten free

INGREDIENTS:

1 fresh purple onion peeled rinsed and sliced

1 medium head of fresh purple cabbage

1/2teaspoon real sea salt

1/3 teaspoon cayenne pepper

1/2 teaspoon garlic powder

1/3 teaspoon paprika powder

1 ripe, but not overly ripe plantain peeled and sliced

2 tablespoons olive oil

DIRECTIONS:

Cut the cabbage into fourths and slice thinly and (freeze the core for a smoothie.

Wash the cut up cabbage and drain well.

Slice the onion and put it in a large pot.

Add drain purple cabbage, seasonings to the pot.

Steam the cabbage covered on high heat on top of the stove until they come to a quick boil. Then stir well to mix in the seasonings and 1/3 cup spring water and reduce heat to medium/low heat and steam for 25 minutes.

Add olive oil and stir.

Add the prepared plantains on top and sprinkle paprika on top and continue cooking for 10 minutes then turn off heat and keep covered until time to serve.

Serve hot as a side dish.

Preparations items needed: large pot, stirring spoon, cutting board, knife, measuring spoons and cups.

Stir fried millet and vegetables

Serves: 8 Preparation Time: 10 minutes Cooking Time: 25 minutes
Total Time: 35 minutes

Description: Stir fry, it is a quick one dish meal with lots of veggies
that is light and satisfying and any veggie you desire to use can be put
in stir fry

INGREDIENTS:

1cup cooked millet

1/2 piece of green bell pepper

3 bok Choy leaves

1chinese cabbage leaf

1small carrot

1onion

3 baby Bella mushrooms

1/2teaspoon garlic powder

1/2 teaspoon grounded ginger

1/8 teaspoon of cayenne pepper

1 tablespoon grounded turmeric powder

2 tablespoons Bragg's liquid amino or to taste

3 tablespoons grape seed oil

1/4 cup spring water

*Cook whole grain millet ahead of time take 20 minutes to cook. Peel and rinse and dry the mushrooms then slice.

Wash and slice the veggies in thin slices with a sharp knife.

Drain well the veggies before stir frying.

Stir fry sliced vegetables and mushrooms in grape seed oil for 3-minute in large sauté pan.

Then add the cooked millet and toss the millet, seasonings and vegetables together.

Once all items are mixed well add 1/4 cup water and cover and steam for 2 minutes and toss.

Take off the heat and sprinkle a little paprika over the top and set aside.

Serve warm.

*Optional: cooked scrambled tofu can be mixed with above recipe. Nutty long grain basmati rice page 101 can be used instead of the healthy whole grain millet page 151 and Scrambled tofu on page 91.

Preparation items needed: measuring cup, large heavy stainless steel sauté pan, large stirring spoon and fork, knife and cutting board.

Paprika string beans and red potatoes

Serves: 8 Preparation Time: 20 minutes Cooking Time: 20 minutes
Total Time: 40 minutes

Description: This recipe is great when you want to cook a one dish
starch and vegetable. It is quick and comforting.

INGREDIENTS:

2pound fresh string beans ends cut off and beans snapped.

4 fresh organic red potatoes cut in cubes with skins on

1 small green bell pepper cored rinsed and cubed

2-tablespoons cold pressed olive oil

1/2 teaspoon real sea salt

2 pinches paprika reserved to sprinkle on top when dish is done

1/4 teaspoon of ground cayenne pepper

1/2cup spring water

1/8 teaspoon garlic powder

DIRECTIONS:

Put all prepared veggies into the pan with the string beans and wash them and let them drain.

Then put all veggies into a large pot.

Add all of the seasonings, water, stir and bring to a boil then steam covered on medium/ low heat on top of the stove for 20 minutes or until potatoes are tender.

Add the oil over the string beans and potatoes.

Turn off heat and sprinkle the paprika on top and leave covered. Serve hot.

*Suggestion: serve as a side dish

Preparation items needed: large pot, cutting board, knife, measuring spoons and cups

Sunflower seeds lentil bean loaf

Serves: 10 Preparation Time: 20 minutes Cooking Time: 1hr +5 minutes Total Time 1hr + 25 minutes:

Description: This savory loaf is a good alternative to meatloaf and can be sliced. And served with fructose free Ketchup, stone ground mustard or tomato gravy

INGREDIENTS:

1 red bell pepper

1 stalk celery

4 garlic cloves

1 carrot

1 medium onion

3 slices of wasa light rye crisp bread

1/2 cup gluten free oats

1-1/3 cups grounded raw sunflower seeds

1/2 cup chopped baby Bella mushrooms

1/3 cup olive oil for sautéing veggies

3 cups cooked drained organic lentils

2 tablespoons grounded flax seeds

1/4 teaspoon cayenne pepper

1/2 tablespoon cilantro

1 tablespoon paprika powder

1 tablespoon grounded thyme

3 tablespoons Bragg's liquid amino

Basting mix:

1/4 cup lentil liquid

1 teaspoon paprika powder

1 teaspoon Bragg's liquid amino

1 teaspoon olive oil

DIRECTIONS:

Cooking the beans:

First, pick out any small rocks or trash rinse well and drain. Cook 1-1/2 cup lentil beans in 4 cups water on high heat to boil then turn heat to medium and cook for 25 minutes or until tender then drain and proceed to make loaf.

Lightly spray baking dish with nonstick spray.

Preheat oven to 375 degrees.

Wash all vegetables well.

Grind bell pepper, celery, carrot and garlic in the food processor and set aside.

Chop the onion small with a knife

Mix the basting mix and set aside.

Grind crisp bread in food processor and set aside.

Grind the sunflower seeds and fennel seeds in food processor to a meal, set aside.

Wash the mushrooms and dry then chop.

Sauté mushrooms, grounded veggies for 3 minutes in 1 teaspoon of olive oil.

Put cooked and drained beans in a large bowl.

Save liquid for later use in soups or gravies.

Mash the beans with a potato masher or food processor until most of the beans are mashed.

Add the chopped onions, sautéed vegetables, flax seed meal and dry seasonings and mix well.

Add liquid amino, oat, grounded sunflower seeds, grounded fennel seeds and grounded bread crumbs to the mixture and mix well.

Put the bean mixture into a prepared dish and shape into loaf with hands.

Pour some of the basting mixture over loaf.

Cover the pan and place in the preheated oven.

Bake in oven for 30 minutes covered then baste and cook 25 minutes uncovered.

Let loaf sit in oven for 5 minute then remove loaf to a cooling board for 5 minutes before serving.

Spicy vegetable gravy

Preparation: large bowl, medium oven proof baking dish with lid, mesh strainer, stirring spoon, tablespoon, measuring cup and spoons, knife, cutting board, food processor and potato masher.

Supreme fennel tofu loaf

Serves: about 14 Preparation Time: 20 minutes Cooking Time: 1 +5 minutes hour Total Time: 1 hour+ 25 minute.

Description: Tofu takes on whatever seasoning that it is cooked with. This loaf is very tasty with spicy vegetable gravy page 225

INGREDIENTS:

1/2 cup pumpkin seeds grounded

1 cup hazelnuts grounded

2 stalks celery

4 cloves garlic

1/2 cup fresh fennel washed and chopped fine

1 red bell pepper

1 green and yellow bell peppers

2 packages firm sprouted tofu

1 cup brown rice flour

2 tablespoons grounded flaxseeds

1/3 cup olive oil

2 tablespoons Bragg's liquid amino

2 teaspoons grounded turmeric

1 teaspoon grounded sage

1 tablespoon grounded rosemary

1 teaspoon cilantro

1 tablespoon paprika powder reserve 1/4 teaspoon for top of loaf

235

1/3 teaspoon chipotle pepper

1/4 teaspoon red pepper seeds

1 can organic olive oil non-stick spray

DIRECTIONS:

Preheat oven at 375 degrees.

Wash all vegetables well.

Spray the baking dish on the bottom and sides with olive oil spray

Ground pumpkin seeds, nuts, celery, garlic in food processor

Rinse and cored the bell peppers.

With a knife chop fine the fresh fennel and half of each bell pepper reserve 4 slices of each bell pepper

Rinse the tofu and pat dry.

In large bowl mash tofu very well with hands.

Add flour, flaxseeds, olive oil and liquid amino, all dry seasons to mixture and add grounded veggies, pumpkin seeds, nuts celery, garlic, chopped veggies and mix together well.

Shape mixture into two loaves and put in prepared baking dish and sprinkle reserved paprika over the loaves and garnish with sliced bell peppers.

Bake for 1 hour until loaves get browned and firm. Turn oven off and let loaves sit in oven for 5 minutes. Take out and let sit for 5 minutes. Serve warm with spicy tomato gravy on page 68

Preparation items needed: large bowl, large, knife, measuring spoon, measuring cup, oblong ovenproof baking dish, potato masher and food Processor.

Ginger curried tofu

Serves: 8 Preparation Time: 10 minutes Cooking Time: 45minutes
Total Time: 55 minutes

Description: Stay lean and fit with tofu. It has lots of calcium, minerals
and vitamins and absorbs spices great.

INGREDIENTS:

1tablespoon grounded ginger powder

1 large fresh tomato

1medium onion

3 Garlic cloves

1stalk of fresh celery

1 teaspoon paprika powder

1/4 teaspoon red pepper seeds

2 tablespoons grounded turmeric

4tablespoons Jamaican curry powder

1/2teaspoon grounded thyme

3 bay leaves, fresh or dried

2 packs extra firm sprouted tofu rinsed and cut in medium cubed.

1/4cup Bragg's liquid amino

3tablespoons cold pressed olive oil

1/2gallon spring water

DIRECTIONS:

Put tomato in boiling hot water for 3 minutes then poke and peel off skin and chop with knife

Wash all vegetables well.

Put onion and garlic in food processor and chop fine

Slice the celery thin with the a sharp knife

Add the oil chopped onions, garlic, celery and seasonings to the pot and sauté for 5 minutes on top of the stove on medium heat.

Add the prepared tofu, tomato, liquid amino and gently mix well.

Continue to sauté for 5 more minutes on medium heat. Stir and add the 2 cups water and let come to a quick boil then lower heat to medium low and cook covered for 35 minutes or until the liquid is like a gravy.

Great over nutty flavored quinoa page 277, millet page 151 or long grain basmati rice page102

Preparation items needed: medium non-stick sauté pot, food processor, stirring spoon, measuring spoons and cup, knife and cutting board.

Swinging Vegan meat balls

Serves: 9 Preparation Time: 20 minutes Cooking Time 1hr + 30 minutes total time: 1 hr+ 50 minutes

Description: These meat balls are made with fresh veggies, seasonings and are delicious

INGREDIENTS:

Grease baking pan well and set aside.

For meat balls

1 onion

3 garlic cloves

1 red bell pepper

4 sprigs fresh parsley

1-1/2cups walnuts

4cups Presoaked textured vegetable protein granules

1/2 cup olive oil

2tablespoons grounded flaxseeds

6 tablespoons spring water

2/3 cup spelt flour

1 tablespoon grounded basil

1 tablespoon grounded oregano

1 tablespoon grounded fennel

1/4 teaspoon whole fennel seeds

1 tablespoon paprika powder

3 tablespoons Bragg's liquid amino

1/2 teaspoon red pepper seeds

Directions for meat balls

Soak protein overnight in large bowl covered with spring water or for 30 minutes in very hot water in a bowl. Squeeze out the water before using. Measure out 4 cups.

Leftover protein can be frozen.

Grind walnuts into a very fine meal in food processor, set aside

Soak flaxseeds in water for 5 minutes in cup

Peel and rinse onion and garlic then chop in food processor, set aside

Rinse the bell pepper and parsley.

Put the bell pepper and parsley in food processor and grind fine, set aside

Put the protein in large bowl.

Add chop onions and garlic, ground veggies, seasonings and liquid amino.

Add olive oil, flax seeds mixture.

Add the flour, walnut meal and mix well.

Shape protein into golf size balls place in oblong baking pan and pour 3/4 cup sauce around the sides of pan.

Bake covered for 30 minutes then uncover and bake for 30 minutes.

Preheat oven 375 degrees

Directions for the sauce:

1 onion and garlic peeled and rinsed and chopped in food processor

2 sprigs of basil de stem and rinsed well chop in food processor

2 tablespoons olive oil

1 tablespoon liquid amino, 1 teaspoon oregano

1/8 teaspoon cayenne pepper

1 tablespoon pure maple syrup, 3 cups spring water

1 tomato soaked in boiling hot water for 3 minutes then peeled.

Put the chopped onion, garlic and basil in a pot on top of the stove then sautéed in olive oil. Mix together liquid amino, oregano, cayenne pepper, pure maple syrup, spring water and tomato paste stir well then add to pot and cook on top of stove for 30 minutes on medium heat. Keep sauce warm for serving over meatball.

Preparation items: large oblong stainless steel baking pan, medium stainless steel pot, food processor, knife, 2 large bowl, large spoon, measuring cup and spoons, and cutting board.

Tangy Lemon frosting

Frost 1 cake Preparation Time: 5minute blending Time 5: minutes
Total Time: 10 minutes

Description: Tangy with the taste of lemon.

INGREDIENTS:

5cups of organic powdered sugar sifted

2 tablespoons soft earth balance spread

2 tablespoons soft earth balance organic vegan shortening

Pinch aluminum free baking soda

1 tablespoon fresh organic lemon juice- save peel to grind

1 tablespoon organic lemon peels grounded very fine optional

DIRECTIONS:

Rinse well the lemon then juice the lemon and strain 1 tablespoon of
lemon juice before adding to the frosting mix.

Finely grind the lemon peel and measure out 1 tablespoon and set aside

Put the sifted powdered sugar and baking soda in a large bowl and add the earth balance, shortening, lemon juice and mix with electric or hand mixer on slow speed or until fluffy

Add a little almond milk if needed until you reach a spread able consistency and mix with electric mixer to make sure all of the lumps are blended and the frosting are creamy and fluffy.

Preparation items: lemon juicer, large bowl, electric mixer, knife, cutting board, measuring spoons and cup.

Decorate the cake top after frosting with the grounded lemon peels

Seasoned tofu French fries

Serves: 4 Preparation Time: 20 minutes Cooking Time: 20 minutes
Total Time: 40 minutes

Description: Flavorful and go well goes with ketchup

I made these fries one evening and my husband said they reminded him of French fries and lo this is it.

INGREDIENTS:

1 teaspoon garlic powder

1 teaspoon onion powder

1 tablespoon grounded turmeric powder

1 tablespoon paprika powder

1/4 teaspoon cayenne pepper

1/2 cup white spelt flour

1 cup olive oil

2-Blocks of extra firm organic sprouted tofu cut in medium strips

1/4cup of Bragg's liquid amino

DIRECTIONS:

Mix the dry seasonings together in a large zip lock bag.

Heat fry pan with half of the olive oil.

Put half of the tofu fries in the bag with the seasonings, flour and toss lightly and place the fries in the fry pan.

Fry on top of the stove on medium heat for 3 minutes then flip over and continue cooking until strips are brown.

Then place the fries on a large plate covered with paper towels to drain.

Continue the process until all of the tofu fries are cooked and golden brown.

Place all of the fries back in the frying pan and sprinkle the liquid amino all over them and toss lightly.

Continue cooking on medium heat until all of the liquid amino is absorbed into the fries.

Remove fries from the pan to the plate with clean paper towels to drain.

Serve hot with ketchup on the side.

Preparation items: large heavy duty non-stick fry pan, measuring cups and spoons, 1 large plate, fork, knife, cutting board pancake flipper and paper towels.

Gluten free tofu pumpkin seed salad

Serves: 5. Preparation Time: 20. Cooking Time: 0. Total Time: 20 minutes.

Description: very refreshing, light and delicious. Make a nice sandwich with lettuce, sprouts and tomatoes or can be served on crackers

INGREDIENTS:

1 block extra firm sprouted tofu rinsed, drained and dry with paper towel

2 tablespoons Bragg's liquid amino or to taste

1/2 cup vegenaise salad spread or more if needed

1 stalk celery

1/3 cup purple onions

1/3 teaspoon parsley flakes

Small piece of carrot grounded

Pinch cayenne pepper

1/2 cup grounded pumpkin seed

1 tablespoon grounded flax seeds

Sprinkle paprika on finish dish

DIRECTIONS:

Wash all vegetables well.

Grind pumpkin seed and flaxseeds in food processor to a fine meal and set aside.

Grind the onion, carrot, celery and garlic in food processor and set aside.

Put the rinsed and dried tofu in a large bowl.

Mash the tofu with a potato masher or hands until crumbly then sauté in a nonstick pan for 5 minutes on medium heat and then remove back to the cleaned bowl.

Add all seasonings, grounded pumpkin seeds and flaxseeds, onions, carrots, garlic, Celery and stir and mash together until well combined.

Sprinkle paprika on top.

Preparation items: medium bowl, potato masher, food processor, cutting board, large spoon and measuring spoons and cup, sharp knife.

Tossed salad supreme

Serves: 3 Preparation Time: 10 minutes Cooking Time: 8 Total Time: 16 minutes

Description: This is a favorite one dish meal. Very colorful and tasty

INGREDIENTS:

5-Leaves of fresh romaine lettuce washed and sliced

2 handful of spring mix rinsed

1 stalk fresh celery rinsed and sliced

1 fresh organic cucumber washed and sliced thin with skin on

2 Roma fresh tomatoes rinsed and cubed

2 avocado washed, peeled and sliced

1 small purple onions peeled rinsed and sliced

Topping:

1 Pack organic extra firm sprouted tofu

1/3cup Bragg's liquid amino

3 tablespoons organic olive oil

1teaspoon turmeric powder

1/2 teaspoon ginger

1 Pinch of cayenne pepper

1/4 teaspoon garlic powder

DIRECTIONS:

Salad:

Put prepared veggies in colander to drain or spin in a salad spinner. Gently toss all veggies together and place in a large bowl and set in refrigerator.

Topping:

Rinse and dry tofu then slice into small cubes

Put the prepared tofu on a nonstick sauté pan. Mix olive oil, turmeric, ginger, cayenne pepper, garlic powder and liquid amino in a cup and spread half over the tofu and sauté. Flip the tofu over and spread the remaining mixture over the tofu and let brown. Serve on top of individual plates of tossed salad topped with raw creamy supreme carrot salad dressing

Preparation items needed: large wash pan or clean sink, colander, salad spinner, large bowl, measuring cups and spoons, knife, sauté pan, paper towels, plastic mixing spoon and cutting board.

Vegan Mellow vanilla pound cake

Serves: 20 Preparation Time: 20 minutes Cooking Time: 45 minutes Total Time: 1-hr + 5 minutes

Description: By trial and error I finely made the prefect and good tasting vegan pound cake. My family and friends love my cake and I know you will to.

INGREDIENTS:

3-1/2cups Organic white spelt flour

2 tablespoons grounded light colored flaxseeds

6 tablespoons spring water

1 teaspoon aluminum free baking soda

2 teaspoon aluminum free baking powder

1/4 teaspoon real sea salt

1-1/3cup soft earth balance margarine

1 cup silken tofu

1/2cup almond milk

2 cups light brown raw vegan sugar

1 teaspoon alcohol free vanilla flavor- frontier brand

1 teaspoon alcohol free coconut flavor- frontier brand

1 can organic nonstick olive oil spray

Parchment paper

DIRECTIONS:

Preheat oven to 350 degrees.

Spray pan a little and line with parchment paper and spray pan lightly with nonstick olive oil spray.

Mix milk and lemon juice together to curdle

Mix flaxseeds and water together let sit for 5 minutes

Sift the flour, baking soda, baking powder, sea salt in a large bowl and mix dry ingredients together well.

Put the margarine, tofu, milk and lemon mixture, sugar in a blender, add a little at a time until blended then add flaxseed mixture and bland well.

Then add flavors and blend well about 30 seconds.

Slowly add the wet ingredients to the flour mixture bowl and mix with large spoon to incorporate.

Continue mixing with electric mixer until all of the wet and dry mixtures are mixed together well.

Pour mixture into prepared pans.

Shake pans to spread batter even.

Bake for 50 minutes then inserted long skewer in center to see if comes out clean. If uncooked batter or crumbs is on tooth pick cook 3-4 minutes and test again.

Cool cake 10 minutes before taking out of pan.

Frost with cream cheese frosting page 103

Preparation items: 2- 8x4 non-stick loaf pans, knife, measuring cup, and spoons, heavy duty blender, 2 large bowls, large mixing spoon and electric mixer

Vegan mushroom gravy

Yield: 1-1/2pint Preparation Time: 5 minutes Cooking Time: 10 minutes Total 15 minutes

Description: Beautiful mushroom gravy that is good over whatever calls for gravy.

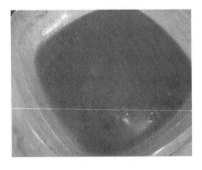

INGREDIENTS:

4 tablespoons spelt flour

2 tablespoons nutritional yeast flakes

1 teaspoon paprika powder

1 Pinch of cayenne pepper powder

1/2 teaspoon onion powder

1 teaspoon garlic powder

1/4 cup sliced mushrooms

4 tablespoons extra virgin olive oil

3 cups vegetable broth page 267 or spring water

3 tablespoons Bragg's liquid amino or to taste

DIRECTIONS:

Put the nutritional yeast, flour, paprika onion powder, garlic powder and cayenne pepper in a small bowl and mix together and set aside.

Put olive oil in fry pan on top of the stove and let it get warm then add the prepare mushrooms and turn the heat to medium and sauté for 2 minutes then put mushrooms in a plate and set aside.

In the same pan add the flour mixture and stir constantly until the flour start to get brown takes 1/2 minutes on medium heat then slowly add 1cup of the broth or water stirring constantly to prevent lumps once everything is mix in and the gravy is gently boiling stir and add the remaining broth.

Add the liquid amino, sautéed mushrooms and stir.

The gravy will be thin at first but continue to cook until the gravy is at desired thickness.

Take10 minutes to thicken on medium low heat.

Taste and add more seasoning if needed

Preparation items needed: large heavy duty sauté pan, measuring cup and spoons, stainless steel whisker or large spoon and knife.

Vegan pineapple coconut cake

Yield 1 cake Preparation Time: 30 minutes Cooking Time: 55 minutes Total Time: 1hour +25 minutes

Description: This cake is very mellow and delicious. It is has lots of coconut and look beautiful. I frosted with cream cheese with coconut sprinkled over the cake and well dried pineapple slices placed on top.

INGREDIENTS:

3-1/2 cups of basic homemade cake flour page292

3 teaspoons aluminum free baking powder

1 teaspoon aluminum free baking soda

1/4teaspoon real sea salt

2 tablespoons grounded golden flaxseeds

6 tablespoons spring water

1-1/3cups soft earth balance buttery spread

1/3cup coconut milk

1/3cup pineapple juice

1 cup drained crushed pineapples

1/2cup easy homemade applesauce-page 7

2 teaspoons alcohol free vanilla flavor

2 cups vegan raw organic light brown cane sugar

DIRECTIONS:

Preheat oven to 350 degrees.

Spray well a nonstick bundt pan with olive oil spray and sprinkle the pan with flour and shake out excess.

Sift the cake flour, baking powder, baking soda and salt into a large bowl.

Mix flaxseeds and water together and let sit for 5 minutes

Put the earth balance spread, coconut milk, pineapple juice, raw sugar, flaxseed mixture, vanilla flavor and applesauce in blender and blend until creamy.

Add the wet mixture to the flour mixture mix in with a large spoon after each addition.

Continue using all of the wet mixture and mixing well

Scrape the sides of bowl.

Add pineapples and continue to mix just enough to blend everything together with electric mixer about 30 seconds.

Pour cake mixture into prepared pan and bake for 55minutes then inserted long wooden skewer in center to see if comes out clean. If uncooked batter or crumbs is on tooth pick cook 3-5 minutes and test again.

Cool 10 minutes before taking out of pan to a plate.

Cool completely before frosting.

Preparation items needed: large non-stick bundt pan, measuring cups and spoons, electric mixer, high speed blender, large spoon, knife, large bowl and cutting board.

Vegan sweet potato pie

Serves: 10 Preparation Time: 1hour + 15 minutes Cooking Time: 45 minutes Total Time: 2 hours

Description: Sweet potato pie that is mellow with a crust that is flaky and taste great and there are less calories in turbinado sugar than in white sugar.

INGREDIENTS:

2 large sweet potatoes about 2 cups

1 cup plus 2 tablespoons organic turbinado sugar in the raw

2/3 cup almond milk

1/2 cup melted earth balance buttery spread

1/2cup spelt flour

1-1/4 teaspoon grounded cinnamon

1/3 teaspoon grounded cloves

1/4 teaspoon of sea salt

1 teaspoons alcohol free vanilla flavor

1/4 teaspoon grounded nutmeg

2 tablespoons grounded light color flaxseeds

6 tablespoons spring water

DIRECTIONS:

Preheat oven 375 degrees

Bake sweet potatoes in the oven until a fork can go in easily about 1 hour.

When the potatoes are cooked and cooled, peel them and put them in the food processor along with the sugar, Margarine, flaxseed mixture, flavor, almond milk and blend until smooth. Add the all dry ingredients a little at a time to the food processor and blend until smooth.

Pour pie filling into prepared pie crusts.

Shake pan a little to even out the pie filling.

Lay parchment paper over pies t help prevent crust from getting to brown.

And bake 45 minutes until crust is light brown and the filling is firm.

Cool completely before serving.

Makes 2- 9 inch pies

Splendid flaky pie crust page 20.

Preparation items needed: large heavy duty pot, food processor, measuring spoons and cups, fork, knife and large spoon.

Delicious vegan sweet potato muffins

Yield 6- 9 muffins Preparation time: 15 minutes cooking time: 36 minutes total time: 56 minutes

Description: very mellow and delicious

INGREDIENTS:

2-1/2 cups spelt flour

1 teaspoon cinnamon

1/2 teaspoon grounded nutmeg

3 teaspoons aluminum free baking powder

1/4teaspoon sea salt

1/2 teaspoon aluminum free baking soda

1cup dried cranberries or raisins optional

1-1/2 cups turbinado sugar in the raw or organic vegan granulated sugar

1-3/4 cups grounded sweet potatoes

1 teaspoon alcohol free vanilla flavoring

2/3 cup grape seed oil

2 tablespoons ground flaxseeds

6 tablespoons warm spring water

1/2cup almond milk

1 teaspoon Bragg's apple cider vinegar

1 can organic nonstick olive oil spray

DIRECTIONS:

Preheat oven to 350 degree

Spray muffin pans with olive oil spray place in unbleached paper muffin cups and set aside

Mix flaxseeds with the water and set aside.

Mix milk and vinegar and set aside.

Put the peel and sliced sweet potato and grind very fine in the food processor and measure out 1-3/4 cups, set aside

Mix thoroughly all dry ingredients (except sugar) in a large bowl.

Mix the sugar, grape seed oil, sweet potato, almond milk mixture, flaxseed mixture and flavor in a blender and blend for 1 minute.

Slowly add the wet ingredients to the dry ingredients and mix with a large spoon just to get everything mixed in well.

Add raisins and mix in well.

Use large spoon to fill muffin pan 3/4 full and bake for 36 minutes.

Check if done by inserting long tooth pick in center to see if comes out clean. If uncooked batter or crumbs is on tooth pick cook 3-4 minutes and test again.

Preparation items needed: large bowl, large measuring cup, measuring cup & measuring spoons, stick free muffin pans, large mixing spoon and heavy duty blender.

Vegetable broth

Serves: 16 Preparation Time: 10 minutes Cooking Time: 1-1/2 hour
Total Time: 1hour +40 minutes

Description: Beautiful amber color that is great wherever broth is
needed

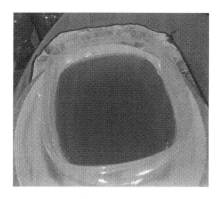

INGREDIENTS:

1/2bunch fresh rosemary

1/2bunch fresh Marjoram

1/2bunch fresh sage

1/2bunch fresh thyme

3 fresh cloves garlic

6 bay leaves, fresh if possible

1 large fresh onion

2 stalks fresh celery

2 large fresh carrots

2 tablespoons Bragg's liquid amino

9 cups spring water

DIRECTIONS:

Peel, wash and clean all of the veggies. Chop the onions, celery, carrots, garlic in medium chunks. Put all prepared veggies in a large heavy duty pot along with the purified water and simmer covered on medium heat on top of the stove for 1-1/2 hours.

Then use a colander to drain broth into a large bowl. Throw away the cooked herbs, save the onions, garlic, celery and carrot to mash and put in the dressing.

Preparation items needed: large heavy duty stainless steel pot, cutting board, large sharp knife, large bowl large jar and colander.

Makes about 8-cups and can be stored in air tight jar for 3 days

Waffle and tofu breakfast sandwich

Serves: 6 Preparation Time: 10 minutes Cooking Time: 15 minutes
Total Time: 25 minutes

Description: These waffles sandwiches are a great morning treat, they are light and delicious.

INGREDIENTS:

1-1/2 cups spelt flour

1/2 cup gluten free buckwheat flour

2 teaspoons aluminum free baking powder

1/2teaspoon aluminum baking soda

Salt optional

1 tablespoon grounded flaxseeds

3 tablespoons spring water

3 tablespoons sweetener of choice

3 cups almond milk

2 tablespoons follow your heart veganaise sandwich spread

3 tablespoons olive oil

1 bottle pure maple syrup

DIRECTIONS:

Preheat waffle iron until green light comes on

Mix flaxseeds mixture, sweetener, olive oil and sandwich spread in blender for 1 second.

Mix dry ingredients in a large measuring cup.

Slowly Pour in wet ingredients and mix until the lumps are dissolved.

It's okay to leave a few of the small lumps.

Let mixture sit for 5 minutes and stir well.

Put 3 tablespoons of waffle mixture on the waffle iron

Close waffle iron and it takes 2 minutes for waffle to cook, green light will come on when done.

Continue until all waffles are made.

Scramble tofu recipe on page 91

Place tofu in between two waffles to make sandwich and pour a little syrup on top and enjoy!

Preparation items: waffle iron cooker, measuring cups and spoons, medium bowl, large bowl, large spoon, serving platter and fork

Happy morning waffles and fruit

Serves: 7 Preparation Time: 15 Cooking Time: 18 minutes Total Time: 33 minutes

Description: Light and delicious with maple syrup and fruit on top

INGREDIENTS:

1-1/2 cups spelt flour

1cup unbleached unenriched and unbromated all-purpose flour

3 teaspoons aluminum free baking powder

1/2 teaspoon aluminum free baking soda

2 generous tablespoons oat bran

Salt optional

1 cup blueberries washed and drained

1/2 cup peeled, rinsed and finely sliced apples

1 tablespoon grounded flaxseeds

3 tablespoons warm spring water

4 tablespoons sweetener of choice-I use pure maple syrup

3 cups almond milk

2 tablespoons follow your heart vegenaise sandwich spread

3 tablespoons olive oil

1 bottle pure maple syrup

DIRECTIONS:

Preheat waffle iron

Mix flaxseeds and water together and let sit for 5 minutes.

Then mix milk, olive oil, flax seed mixture, sweetener and sandwich spread in blender for 1 second.

Mix dry ingredients in a large measuring cup.

Slowly Pour in wet ingredients and mix until most of the lumps are dissolved.

It's okay to leave a few of the small lumps.

Let mixture sit for 5 minutes and stir well.

Put 3 generous tablespoons on the waffle iron and spread out.

Close waffle iron and it takes 2 minutes for waffle to cook.

Continue until all waffles are made.

Variety: different fruit can be used or sprinkled with organic powdered sugar

Serve hot with fruit and maple syrup on top.

Preparation items: nonstick waffle iron cooker, measuring cups and spoons, medium bowl, large bowl, large spoon, serving platter and fork.

Warm up your tummy cheesy yellow grits

Serves: 4 Preparation Time: 5 minutes Cooking Time: 25 minutes Total Time: 30 minutes

Description: This is a southern flair dish that is versatile and yummy that will makes you hungry. I added cheese with the grits and served with toast and scrambled tofu on the side and this meal is gluten free.

Grits is an old family favorite we would cook grits for the family with all the trimmings on Sunday mornings. I love to cook grits on cool mornings for my family but I changed some of the trimmings.

INGREDIENTS:

1cup organic gluten free yellow grits

4 cups spring water

1/2 teaspoon sea salt

1/4cup diaya cheddar cheese grated in food processor

1 loaf gluten free bread

1 stick of earth balance spread

DIRECTIONS:

Put the grits in a small holed strainer and rinse well.

Put 3 cups of water in a medium pot and bring to a boil takes about 4 minutes.

Then whisk in the grits slowly and continue to whisk until the grits are mix in with the water and starts to cook and there are no lumps.

Cover and cook on medium/ low heat for 20 minutes stirring often to prevent lumps.

Add more water if needed and when the grits are creamy then add the salt and 1 tablespoon earth balance spread, cheese and stir.

Serve hot with scrambled tofu and toast on the side.

Varieties: purple onions and green, red peppers can be rinsed and chopped and sautéed and added on the side. Milk and sugar and a pinch of cinnamon can be added to a bowl of grits if desired.

Preparation items: medium heavy duty stainless steel pot with lid, large nonstick sauté pan, measuring cup and spoons, large spoon, chopping board, knife and food processor

Recipe for scrambled tofu

Yummy vegan banana pudding

Serves: 6 Preparation Time: 25 minutes Cooking Time: 10 minutes
Total Time: 35 minutes

Description: beautiful pudding and taste great

INGREDIENTS:

1/2 teaspoon cinnamon

2 teaspoons vanilla flavor

5 ripe bananas

2 boxes vanilla cookies by nature path

2-2/3 cups almond milk

3 tablespoons non- genetically modified corn starch or potato starch

4-1/2 tablespoons vegan sugar

1 can vegan whipped cream optional

DIRECTIONS:

Preheat oven to 350 degrees

Step 1 making the pudding

In a small bowl, whisk together 2/3 cups almond milk and cornstarch and making sure to whisk out lumps and set aside.

Put remaining milk, cinnamon and sugar in a small pot over medium heat and whisk together.

When mixture begins to get hot, Wisk in the cornstarch mixture and stir well.

Whisk constantly while cooking until mixture begins to bubble this takes about 5 minutes.

Turn down heat to low and add well mashed banana cook 4 minutes more and whisking constantly.

Turn off heat and add vanilla extract and stir well.

Step 2 making the banana pudding

Save 8 of the broken cookie and crumbs for the topping.

Line the bottom of a round oven proof dish with the vanilla cookies then generously slice bananas on top of the cookies and spoon in some of the pudding over the bananas. Continue this process and end with pudding on top of the bananas.

Step 3 making the topping.

Put the saved cookies in the blender and crush the cookies to make crumbs. Sprinkle the crumbs over the top of the banana pudding.

Step 4 Baking.

Bake in the oven for 10 minutes then remove and let pudding cool completely in refrigerator. Serve with whip cream topping.

Preparation items: Medium stainless steel pot, stirring spoon, measuring spoons and cup, knife, heavy duty blender and heat resistant oblong Pyrex dish.

Zesty quinoa and red bell peppers

Serves: 4 Preparation time: 5 minutes Cooking Time: 20 Total Time: 25 minutes

Recipe Description: colorful and very tasty. Quinoa is a good source of complete protein

I use this dish in the place of rice. It is gluten free and extremely healthy.

INGREDIENTS:

1cup quinoa

1-1/4cups spring water

1tablespoon extra virgin olive oil

1/3 piece of red bell pepper

2tablespoons Bragg's liquids amino

1/3teaspoon cayenne pepper or to taste

1/3 teaspoon basil flakes

1 sprig of fresh fennel or 1/3 teaspoon fennel flakes

DIRECTIONS:

Wash and drain the quinoa in a strainer with small holes

Rinse the bell pepper and cube.

Put water on stove and let come to a boil

Add the drained quinoa, cubed peppers, fresh fennel and seasonings.
Turn the heat to low and steam covered on the stove for 20 minutes.

Test a grain for doneness if not done add 1/3cup water and continue to cook covered for 5 minutes.

Turn off the heat and fluff with a fork and let sit covered for 5 minutes then fluff again and take out fennel sprig.

Preparation items: strainer with small holes, measuring cup and spoons, cutting board, knife, medium pot with lid.

Nutty flavored quinoa

Serves: 4 Preparation Time: 5 minutes Cooking Time: 20 minutes Total Time: 25 minutes

Description: Quinoa is a healthy dish to serve. It has a nutty flavor and is considered a complete protein. Good replacement for rice

INGREDIENTS:

1 cup quinoa rinsed well and drained in a mesh strainer

1-3/4cups spring water

1 tablespoon Bragg's liquid amino or 1/3 tsp sea salt

1 tablespoon earth balance buttery spread

DIRECTIONS:

Pour in 1-3/4 cups of fresh water and add the liquid amino and earth balance spread and bring water to a boil.

Drain off the rinsing water with small holed mesh strainer and add prepared quinoa to the hot water.

Turn heat to low and steam covered on top of the stove for 20 minutes. Test a grain for doneness and if needed add 1/4 cup water and steam for another 5 minutes and leave covered.

Do not fluff until all of the water is absorbed. Turn off heat and fluff the quinoa and leave covered.

Serve hot as a side dish to replace rice or you can use it in a stir fry dish.

Preparation item needed: medium size heavy duty stainless steel pot with lid, small holed mesh strainer, stirring spoon, measuring spoons and cups and fork

Vegan cream of wheat bread

Serves: Preparation Time: 11 minutes Cooking Time: 45 minutes
        Total Time: 56 minute

Recipe Description: This beautiful bread is a good replacement for corn bread. Cream of wheat is light and easy to digest.

INGREDIENTS:

3cups Sooji fine cream of wheat

1/4teaspoon sea salt

3 teaspoons aluminum free baking powder

2 tablespoons grounded flax seeds

6 tablespoons spring water

3-1/2 cups cold original almond milk

1/3 cup vegan sour cream

1/2 teaspoon grounded turmeric

1/4cup organic olive oil

2 tablespoons raw maple syrup

1/4 cup raisins- optional

Non-stick organic coconut spray

DIRECTIONS:

Prepare 9 inch deep glass baking pan by greasing pan with olive oil nonstick spray.

Preheat oven to 400 degrees

Soak flaxseeds in 6 tablespoons spring water for 5 minutes.

273

Combine all dry ingredients in a large bowl and mix well.

Stir in 2-1/2 cups milk, sour cream, flaxseed mixture and mix well

Add the maple syrup, raisins and olive oil and mix really well about 10 seconds.

Let mixture sit for 5 minutes.

Stir in the last of milk adding a little at a time and stirring until the consistency is loose and fluffy and mixed well.

Pour mixture into prepared 9 inch deep glass baking dish. Sprinkle a tsp of olive oil over the top

Bake for 45 minutes or until light brown and feel firm.

Tip: cover bread to keep soft after baking.

9 large muffins can be made from this recipe but spray the muffin pan with nonstick spray and put water in unused muffin holes. Bake for 25 minutes and the muffins are light brown and the tops feel firm.

Preparation items needed: oven proof glass baking dish, lid, large bowl, measuring spoons and cups, mixing spoons, toothpicks, large muffin pans.

Paradise flatbread sandwiches

Serves: 5 Preparation Time: 20 minutes Cooking Time: 5 minutes
Time: 35 minutes

Description: These wrap sandwiches taste great anytime. They are quick to make and make a quick meal on weekends.

INGREDIENTS:

1/4cup olive oil

1/2 teaspoon garlic powder

1/8 teaspoon real sea salt
Hot pepper seeds optional

8 leaves of organic purple tipped lettuce

2 fresh organic cucumbers

2 large fresh organic tomatoes

1 purple onion

1 package organic alfalfa sprouts

2 medium firm organic avocado

1 package diaya vegan cheese

1 tablespoon Bragg's liquid amino

1 package whole wheat flatbread bread

Long wooden tooth pick

DIRECTIONS:

Preheat oven to 400 degree

Mix the olive oil, garlic powder, hot pepper seeds and liquid amino together and set aside.

Wash and slice thin the lettuce, tomatoes, cucumber and onion.

Soak alfalfa sprouts in water for 5 minutes then rinse and drain.

Put prepared lettuce, tomatoes, cucumbers, onion and alfalfa sprouts in salad spinner and spin to dry vegetables- set aside.

Rinse the avocado.

Tip- to peel avocado, slice the peeling into sections, then peel.

Place prepared avocado on paper towel placed in bowl.

Crumble up vegan cheese in food processor and place in a bowl. Set aside.

Lay the 5 flatbreads on flat surface and put the veggies on the flat bread and end with the cheese and sprinkle on a little of the olive oil mixture. Fold the flatbread and put in tooth pick to hold bread together and place sandwiches on a cookie sheet and put in hot oven for 5 minutes. Take out of the oven and serve warm.

Preparation items needed: cutting board, sharp knife, cookie sheet 3 medium bowls, food processor and 2 plates

Vegan black molasses cookies

Yields 28 or 30 medium cookies Preparation Time: 15 minutes
Cooking Time: 10 minutes per batch Total Time: 45 minutes

Description: Soft and chewy, not overly sweet and very nutritious. Molasses is the dark, sticky syrup left behind after the sugar has been boiled out of sugar cane.

375 preheated oven

Cover cookie sheets with parchment paper and grease lightly.

INGREDIENTS:

2-1/2cups spelt flour

3 tablespoons gluten free coconut flour

1 teaspoon aluminum free baking powder

1 teaspoon aluminum free baking soda

1/4 teaspoon sea salt optional

1 teaspoon cinnamon

1/2 teaspoon nutmeg

1/2cup organic rolled oatmeal

1/2cup Brazil nut chopped

2/3 cup olive oil

1 teaspoons alcohol free real vanilla flavor

2 tablespoons grounded flax seeds mixed in 6 tablespoons spring water

2/3 cup organic light agave nectar

3 tablespoons unsulfured blackstrap molasses

1/3 cup vegan sugar

2 tablespoons almond milk

Parchment paper

Non-stick organic spray

DIRECTIONS:

Finely chop Brazil nuts and set aside

Put the flour, oats, sea salt, baking soda, baking powder, cinnamon, nutmeg and grounded Brazil nuts in a bowl and stir well.

Put olive oil, flavor, agave nectar, sugar, molasses and flax seed mixture in blender and blend well.

Then add the wet mixture to the flour mixture and mix with a large spoon until everything is moist and mixed.

Spray small ice cream scooper or large spoon with non-stick spray and scoop cookie dough and drop onto the cookie sheet. Continue until all cookies are place on cookie sheet. Optional- press cookies dough lightly with lightly sprayed bottom of a plastic cup and even edges with hands.

Space them apart.

Bake cookies 10 minutes each batch.

Let cookies cool for 5 minutes then remove from parchment paper.

Use wax paper between each layer of cookies to prevent them from sticking together when placing in a container.

Preparation items: large bowl, cookie sheets, parchment paper, measuring cups and spoons, blender, small cookie scooper, tablespoon, wax paper and Food processor.

Barbeque no beef bites stew

Serves: 10 Preparation Time: 8 minutes Cooking Time: 50 minutes
Total Time: 58 minutes

Description: Gluten free no beef bites is very tender and delicious and complements any dish. Always soak enough for freezing.

INGREDIENTS:

3cups presoaked no beef bites protein tips

1 stalk of fresh celery

4 garlic cloves

1medium onion

4 tablespoons grape seed oil

1/8 teaspoon red pepper seeds or more if desired

3cups homemade orange barbeque sauce - recipe on page 26

1 teaspoon cinnamon

2 tablespoons Bragg's liquid amino

1/2 gallon spring water

DIRECTIONS:

For fast soaking, soak no beef protein for 30 minutes in boiling hot water and squeeze out water

Peel and rinse garlic and onion.

Rinse celery.

Put celery, garlic, onion in food processor and chopped fine.

Put the protein in a large pot and add the prepared veggies, oil and all of the seasonings and sauté for 3 minutes. Add 2 cups water bring to a boil on high heat on top of the stove then turn heat to medium/low and cook covered for 20 minutes.

Add 3 cups of barbeque sauce and cook covered on low heat for 30 minutes.

Taste and add more seasonings if desired.

Serve over cooked long grain basmati rice page 101 or any cooked grain or noodles.

Preparation items: large stainless steel pot, stirring spoon, large bowl, measuring spoons and cup, knife and cutting board.

Red beans and rice

Serves: 6 Preparation Time: 5 minutes cooking time 1hour and 30 minutes Total time 1 hour +35minutes\

Description: Healthy red beans and rice have lots of fiber, protein and is delicious. I always cook up lots of beans and freeze them so I will always have them on hand when I need them.

INGREDIENTS:

1-1/2 cups presoaked red beans

1 teaspoon grounded thyme

1 small Scot bonnet pepper very hot only use only a small one

1/2 onion

Small piece fresh ginger

3 fresh garlic cloves

3 tablespoons Bragg's liquid amino

3 cups spring water

+Add these items below after the beans are done.

1-1/2 cups organic coconut milk

Bean liquid and spring water mixed together to make 1-1/2 cups

2 tablespoons earth balance spread

2 cups long grain brown basmati rice

++Cooking the beans

First, pick out any small rocks or debris then soak in spring water and 1 teaspoon aluminum free baking soda overnight then drain and rinse well. Measure out 1-1/2 cups of presoaked beans and freeze leftover beans.

DIRECTIONS:

Peel and rinse onion and garlic then chop in food processor.

Peel and rinse ginger.

Rinse the rice then soak the rice for 6 minutes in a bowl drain and set a side.

Put the beans, thyme, Scot bonnet pepper, Liquid amino, onion, fresh ginger and garlic cloves into the pot with the beans and 3 cups water. Cook on top of the stove on high heat until began to boil then turn the heat to medium and cook for 1 hour or until beans are tender. Let the beans cook down low then drain off liquid and save. Take out ginger and Scot bonnet and discard.

Add the earth balance spread, coconut milk, bean liquid and water mixture to the pot and let come to a boil then add presoaked rice and stir. Turn the heat to low and cover the pot and steam the rice until tender. Add a little of water if needed. Take about 25minutes. Serve warm.

Preparation items: medium stainless steel pot with lid, measuring spoons and cups, large bowl, tablespoon knife and cutting board.

Canadian speckle beans dump soup

Serves: 8 Preparation Time: 10 minutes Cooking Time: 1 hour +15minutes Total Time1hr + 25 minutes

Description: It's healthy and hearty and a feel good soup. I wanted to make soup and didn't know what kind to make so I started to dump different fresh veggies and other items that I had on hand in the soup pot and it turned out very good.

INGREDIENTS:

1 small onion

2 garlic cloves

1 organic stalk of celery

1 organic carrot

10 fresh string beans

3tomatoes

1 ear of fresh corn

1 cup organic rotini macaroni

1 cup Canadian speckle beans

1 cup textured vegetable protein beef chips

1 teaspoon grounded turmeric

1/2teaspoon basil flakes

1-1/2 tablespoons smoked paprika

3 tablespoons Bragg's liquid amino

1/3teaspoon cayenne pepper

2 tablespoons olive oil

1 gallon spring water

1 teaspoon aluminum free baking soda

DIRECTIONS:

Pick out debris and soak the beans overnight in purified water and 1/4-teaspoon aluminum free baking soda. Measure out 1 cup of beans and freeze leftover beans.

Soak beef chips in water overnight and squeeze out water from chips before using and freezing. Measure out 1 cup of protein.

Peel, rinse onion, and garlic and grind very fine in food processor and set aside. Wash and sliced celery and carrot and put them in a bowl and set aside.

Wash the string beans and cut ends off and cut into medium pieces and set aside.

Soak the tomatoes in boiling hot water for 3minutes then peel off skin. Cube the tomatoes and set aside.

Peel and de silk the corn and cut the corn off the cob and set aside.

Measure out 1cup rotini and set aside.

Put one cup of presoaked beans, no beef chips and all dry ingredients in a large pot. Add oil, grounded onions, garlic and tomatoes to the pot along with the liquid amino and Sauté for 5 minutes. Stir often.

Add 6 cups water and cook on medium heat on top of the stove for 1 hour or until beans and no beef chips are tender.

When the beans and no beef chips are tender add the corn, string beans, celery, carrots and cook for 10 minutes.

Add the rotini more seasoning and water if needed then cook for 10 minutes more. Serve hot.

Preparation items: large heavy stainless pot, knife, measuring spoons and cup, 2 medium deep bowls, cutting board, stirring spoon, food processor and colander.

Back to basic home-made cake flour

Yield 3-1/2 cups cake flour Preparation time: 10 minutes sifting time

5 minutes total time 15minute

Description: Soft and light cake flour.

INGREDIENTS:

2-3/4cups sifted Bob's red mills organic unbleached unenriched and unbromated all-purpose flour and measure out 2-3/4 cups. 3 tablespoons sifted coconut flour gluten free and measure out 3 tablespoons. Leftover flours can be put back in the bags.

1/2 cup organic bob red mills unmodified potato starch, sift the starch and measure out 1/2cup. Leftover starch can be put back in the bag.

DIRECTIONS:

Sift the flours and starch together with a small holed strainer two times into a large bowl to evenly distribute the mixture.

Now proceed with whatever cake you want to make.

This recipe can be made up and stored in an airtight container.

Remember the more that this mixture is sifted the finer incorporated.

Preparation items needed: measuring cups and spoons, large strainer with small holes and two large bowls.

Power pack green smoothie

Serve5 preparation time: 10 minutes mixing time: 5 minutes total time 15 minutes

Description: Beautiful green and tasty

INGREDIENTS:

2 cups fresh spinach

1 cup fresh parsley

1 apple

1 banana

1/2 stalk celery

2 tablespoons grounded golden flaxseeds

1/2teaspoon grounded turmeric

1-1/2 teaspoons grounded cumin

1 tablespoon flaxseed oil

3 tablespoons golden agave nectar- optional

2 cups spring water

DIRECTIONS:

Fill the blender with half of the ingredients and add the water and blend. Keep the fruit and veggies pushed down into the blender until well blended. Add the other half of the ingredients and continue to blend until creamy.

If the smoothie is too thick add a little water and blend, then Enjoy!!

Serve at once or store in refrigerator. Smoothie will last for 2 days in refrigerator.

Preparation items: heavy duty blender, measuring cups and spoons, knife and cutting board

Yeast & baking powder free spelt loaf bread

Yield 1 loaf Preparation time20 minutes cooking time 1hr +5 minutes total time 1hr +25 minutes

Description; great tasting and hearty loaf of bread

INGREDIENTS:

3-1/2 cups spelt flour

1 teaspoon aluminum free baking soda

1/4-teaspoon real sea salt

2tablespoons grounded flax seeds

6 tablespoons spring water

1 cup raisins or currants

1/2 cup spring water

3/4 cup dried apple slices

1/2cup spring water

1/4 cup grounded raw pumpkin

1/3cup grounded walnuts

1-1/3 cups almond milk

In a medium bowl mix well the flour, baking soda and sea salt and grounded pumpkin seeds and walnuts together.

Mix water and flaxseeds together and set aside.

Grind pumpkin seeds and walnuts and set aside.

Soak raisins in the water for 20 minutes - save the water.

Soak dried apple slices in the water for 20 minutes - save the water.

Drain the raisins and dried apples and set aside. Save the water from the drained raisins and apples.

Add the drained raisins, apples and 1-1/3 cups milk in the blender and blend well. Add flaxseed mixture and blend lightly. Add enough milk to the saved water to balance out to 1 cup and add to the blender and mix lightly. Slowly pour wet mixture into the dry mixture and mix just enough to incorporate everything together. Pour mixture into prepared pan and shake pan to even out the mixture. Bake covered with pan of equal size and bake for 1 hour and 5 minutes or until tester comes out clean. Let the loaf cool for 5 minutes then remove from pan to a plate then enjoy!

Preparation Items: large bowl, measuring cups and spoons, large spoon, knife, blender and 2- 9x5 loaf pans.

Applesauce drizzle frosting

Yield 1-1/2 cups Preparation Time: 15 minutes cooking Time: 10 minutes Total Time: 25minutes

Description beautiful, flavorful and clear frosting

INGREDIENTS:

1/3 cup easy homemade applesauce recipe page7

1cup organic raw light brown sugar

1 cup spring water

1 tablespoon melted earth spread

1 teaspoon alcohol free vanilla flavor

DIRECTIONS:

In a small pot on top of the stove mix the sugar and water and stir with a wooden spoon while cooking the mixture on high heat until start to bubble and thicken take 5 minutes. When the mixture thickens add the applesauce earth balance spread and vanilla flavor and continue to cook and stir for 5 more minutes. Poke a few holes in the cake with a long tooth pick and drizzle the frosting with a spoon over the warm cake.

Let the drizzled cake cool then drizzle some more of the drizzle over the cake. Top with chopped nuts if desired. Or put drizzle frosting in refrigerator to use later if desired.

Preparation items: small pot, stirring spoon, measuring cups and spoons and large wooden spoon.

Made in the
USA
Lexington, KY